"*Sacrilege* is a refreshing book for those c who want to make Jesus known. Hugh Halt book he shares with us how to remove the l meet Jesus in us. *Sacrilege* is a handbook for ...ssional life, but a truly incarnational life. I recommend thi. ...i every Christ follower."
—**Dave Ferguson**, lead pastor, Community Christian Church; spiritual entrepreneur, NewThing

"I can't say anything as clever or thought-provoking as this book that I'm trying to endorse. All I can say is that Hugh, in his fabulously engaging way, accomplishes the release of Christian theology from its church-centric focus back onto the streets—where it got its start and where it belongs. It's like opening a window in a musty room to let in some fresh air."
—**Reggie McNeal**, missional leadership specialist, The Leadership Network

"Hugh Halter has written a carefully constructed theological Molotov cocktail, which explodes false myths while it fires up the Christian imagination for truth, beauty, and goodness."
—**Leonard Sweet**, bestselling author and professor at Drew University and George Fox University

"This book *is* Hugh Halter the man: irreligious, forthright, honest, fun, insightful, creative, adventurous, and compassionate. And so it is an insightful, practical, missional guide to the *sacrilegious* life of those who want to follow Jesus in the way he wants to be followed—sacrilegiously."
—**from the foreword by Alan Hirsch**, author of various books including *Untamed; Right Here, Right Now;* and *The Faith of Leap*

"I know Hugh Halter. He is a nonconformist, a dissenter, an iconoclast, and a rabble-rouser. He's also a deeply compassionate man who has opened his home, his life, and his heart to the lost, the lonely, the disillusioned, and the infuriated. Here is a book about the sacrilegious Jesus written by a humble man who knows him, *really* knows him, and who has sought to emulate his work in our broken world. He must be listened to."
—**Michael Frost**, author or coauthor of *ReJesus*, *The Faith of Leap*, and *The Road to Missional*

"I love Hugh Halter's sense of adventure and living in the moment. That is exactly what *Sacrilege* is about—living in the moment, following Jesus, letting our relationship with Jesus push the boundaries out. Hugh is not an ivory tower writer but a trekker out on the range who goes from descending into the hot, sweaty, dense jungle to climbing high in the dry cold to summit mountains. It's time to shake up our notions about what a disciple is and what it really means to follow Jesus. Hugh is one of the few who does just that."
—**Bob Roberts**, pastor and author of *Transformation* and *Glocalization*

"Yet again, Hugh tips the sacred cows that need tipping and ruffles the feathers that need ruffling. This isn't done through hyperbole or distortion but through a genuine examination of Jesus's life. Some will decide this is a controversial book, but in fact, Jesus was a controversial Savior. This is simply an honest retelling of Jesus's unruly story with a simple call to be like him in a world where most prefer their cows untipped and their feathers unruffled."

—**Jen Hatmaker**, speaker and author of nine books, including *Interrupted* and *Seven*

"Every once in a while someone comes along who seems to speak your personal language. They give words to things you have struggled to articulate yourself. My friend Hugh Halter is one of those people, and *Sacrilege* is one of those books that makes you want to read one more chapter though the clock says it's time to go to bed. If you think you have heard all that Hugh has to say to the body of Christ, you are wrong. This is another gutsy and entertaining book by a genuine Jesus guy."

—**Lance Ford**, coauthor of *Right Here, Right Now*

"Halter's done it with *Sacrilege*. He's somehow managed to write a book that brings everything into alignment for those who are trying to follow Jesus without all the mess. This riveting book will give you a fresh vision for your life and the world."

—**Carl Medearis**, author of *Muslims, Christians, and Jesus*; *Tea with Hezbollah*; and *Speaking of Jesus*

"In *Sacrilege*, Hugh Halter attacks our spiritual sensibilities with a jarringly honest appraisal of the church. He also (to use even more street slang) 'takes us to church'—specifically the church Jesus would attend. Halter is a missional apostle cut out of the same cloth as Saint Patrick. He is wild about Jesus, bullish about outsiders, and, despite numerous misgivings, still willing to stay connected with the church. Given Hugh's low expectations (he only needs to convince three of us in order to feel successful), he only needs two more of you to sign up."

—**Jim Henderson**, author of *Jim and Casper Go to Church* and coauthor of *The Outsider Interviews*

"Every generation God compels a handful of courageous leaders—prophets— to call the church back to its Jesus movement essence. Hugh Halter is such a leader. In *Sacrilege*, Hugh compels the church to ask a very dangerous question behind everything it does: 'Why?' For the sake of Christ and all those he lived and died and lived again to save, I dare you to step into that space, read the book, and do as God and his Scriptures lead—nothing more, nothing less."

—**Jim Mellado**, Willow Creek Association

"Raise a glass! Here's to shaking away any and all 'religion' and setting Jesus free to be who he is, the One who loves and pursues us relentlessly! Finally a book that speaks to the radical and countercultural way of Jesus in a way that is true, honest, and compelling to my friends who have given up on faith and to my friends who are desperate to find it."

—**Brad Corrigan**, member of the band Dispatch

SACRILEGE

THE SHAPEVINE MISSIONAL SERIES

ORGANIC LEADERSHIP
Neil Cole

THE FAITH OF LEAP
Michael Frost and Alan Hirsch

THE ROAD TO MISSIONAL
Michael Frost

SACRILEGE
Hugh Halter

UNTAMED
Alan Hirsch and Debra Hirsch

RIGHT HERE, RIGHT NOW
Alan Hirsch and Lance Ford

ROOTED IN GOOD SOIL
Tri Robinson

SACRILEGE

FINDING LIFE IN THE UNORTHODOX WAYS OF JESUS

HUGH HALTER

BakerBooks

a division of Baker Publishing Group
Grand Rapids, Michigan

Published by Baker Books
a division of Baker Publishing Group
P.O. Box 6287, Grand Rapids, MI 49516-6287
www.bakerbooks.com

Printed in the United States of America

Library of Congress Cataloging-in-Publication Data
Halter, Hugh, 1966–
    Sacrilege : finding life in the unorthodox ways of Jesus / Hugh Halter.
        p.   cm. — (Shapevine)
    Includes bibliographical references.
    ISBN 978-0-8010-1359-1 (pbk.)
    1. Jesus Christ—Example. 2. Christian life. I. Title.
BT304.2.H354 2011
232.9′04—dc23   2011020292

11 12 13 14 15 16 17   7 6 5 4 3 2 1

To Alli and McKenna,
that you may find the Jesus I found

CONTENTS

Contents

ABOUT THE SHAPEVINE MISSIONAL SERIES

The key purpose of Shapevine the organization is to bring the various elements of missional Christianity—namely, church planting movements, urban mission, the emerging church, the missional church movement, the organic/simple church, and marketplace ministries—into meaningful dialogue around the truly big ideas of our time. Consistent with this purpose, the Shapevine Missional Series in partnership with Baker Books seeks to bring innovative thinking to the missional issues of church planting, mission, evangelism, social justice, and anything in between.

We seek to publish both established authors as well as others who have significant things to contribute but have operated largely under the radar.

The series will focus on three distinctive areas:

- **Living—Practical Missional Orthopraxy**
  Orthopraxy is what makes orthodoxy worth having. We yearn for the experience and continual flow of living out the gospel message in our day-to-day lives for the sake

of others. The stories and ideas in the Shapevine Missional Series are aimed at providing practical handles and means to wrap our readers' minds around the idea of living as the people of God, sent into the world with the Spirit and impulse of Jesus himself.

- **Learning—Solid Missional Orthodoxy**

  Jesus both lived and proclaimed a theology of a missional God. His was and is a message of mercy, justice, and goodness toward others. It was this message that erupted into the greatest movement in the history of humankind. The same God who sent his only Son now sends those who follow his Son, in the same manner and with the same message. This is at the heart of a missional theology.

- **Leading—Tools for Missional Leadership**

  Our aim is for the books in this series to serve as tools for pastors, organizational leaders, and church members throughout the world to equip themselves and others as they travel the path of faithfulness in the missional life.

As a global interactive forum, Shapevine allows anyone to both learn and contribute at whatever level suits. To learn more, go to www.shapevine.com or contact us at info@shapevine.com.

Alan Hirsch and Lance Ford

SERIES EDITOR'S PREFACE

This is the second Shapevine book focusing on a missional form/interpretation of the discipleship task, the first being that of Debra Hirsch and myself in *Untamed*. This definitely fits the category and the focus of the Shapevine series. You see, Hugh can't help himself. He is an inveterate missionary and evangelist, and for some odd reason he really thinks we should all be that way. And so when it comes to writing on discipleship, it was inevitable that he would view this dimension of the Christian experience through that lens. But in my opinion, for what it's worth, this is perhaps the only true lens by which we can understand what it means to authentically follow Jesus. In fact, I believe that a real part of the problem of much of what we call Christianity in our day is that it has failed to see the Great Commission as a call to "make disciples of all nations" (Matt. 28:19) with all that this means (disciples + nations = missional discipleship).

For far too long now we have conceived of discipleship in nonmissional terms. We have tended to locate it in what we call "the spiritual disciplines," comprised of prayer, worship, Bible study, fasting, community life, and so on. In applying the adjective *missional* to the noun of *discipleship*, we want to change the quality as well as the expectations of what is meant by the term discipleship. *Missional* discipleship certainly requires that we keep doing the personal disciplines, but it requires that we practice these within a broader context of our missional calling to those around us. The disciple is meant to be someone who makes a difference in the world—Jesus intended and designed us to be this way. To be a disciple of Jesus is to be a fully empowered agent of the King.

Furthermore, and perhaps more seriously, we have limited the impact and meaning of Christianity by majoring on personal salvation given to us in and through *Jesus as Redeemer* while effectively leaving the *Jesus as Lord* part out of the equation. We buy into the saving work of Jesus big-time, but we dodge his words and his life as prototypical for the authentic Christian life. Talk about a modern-day heresy! As if in a truly biblical faith you could have the one without the other! Missional discipleship not only takes the saving work of Jesus seriously, it takes his life seriously as well.

This is a deeply sacrilegious book, and I expect that many will find it offensive. But I think that they will be offended in the right way; that is, the same way that Jesus offended people. Part of the mission of Jesus (and by extension his church) is to relieve us of the intolerable burden of our neo-pharisaic religion. I call it neo-pharisaic because it is just a new manifestation of a disease that has always plagued people of faith—religion! Religion is comprised of laying burdens on people's shoulders, hypocrisy and double standards, gracelessness toward "sinners," high-minded judgmentalism, straining at gnats and swallowing camels, externalization of faith in religious ritual, and not being pure in heart, among other things.

If we evangelicals have need for deliverance from the prevailing sin of our day, it is from the sins of religiosity that we need it most. And praise God, this is exactly what Jesus the Lord and Savior wants to do. In fact, it is what he has always done. And if you doubt this, all you need to do is to track the ministry of our Master. Just read Matthew 21–23 to get the power of the sacrilegious message of Jesus. He reserves his harshest possible criticisms not for the sinners of his day but rather for religious people. Heck, he's just out-and-out offensive when it comes to religiosity!

I have to confess that I really love Hugh Halter. I consider him a dear friend and a wonderful example of missional discipleship and activism. And few are better equipped to deliver a prophetic restatement of the message and implications of Jesus's life than the sacrilegious Hugh-Dog Halter. As you will soon see, Hugh lives this stuff. If you were to be a fly on the wall of Hugh's life, as I have been, you would see a very messy, almost driven, but always Christlike spirituality at work. This book *is* the man: irreligious, forthright, honest, fun, insightful, creative, adventurous, and compassionate.

And so when Hugh writes, the result is an insightful, practical, missional guide to the *sacrilegious* life of those who want to follow Jesus in the way he wants to be followed—sacrilegiously.

Fasten your seat belt and prepare to be de-religiousified.

Alan Hirsch
Shapevine series editor

ACKNOWLEDGMENTS

The Gospel

After acknowledging in previous books so many people who have influenced my life and my understanding of God, for this book I simply want to acknowledge the gospel as my primary inspiration.

The gospel, or "Good News," is the message of Jesus about a new way of life that he called the kingdom of God. Because of his sinless life, he was able to die for the sins of the world, and thus a new way of existence would now be accessible or tangible to anyone hoping to be reborn spiritually, mentally, socially . . . holistically.

The gospel of his kingdom came first as a simple message, and this message quickly spread. People's jaws would drop when they heard it, and they would drop their nets—and their religious orientations—and follow. The message of the gospel was powerful then, and it still is today. But the gospel is much more than just a message about what comes after life. It is about life now.

That life is embodied in the person of Jesus. He didn't just come to share a concept of good news—he came to show us what the good news of his kingdom looks, feels, and tastes like. The kingdom of God is how things are in heaven. It's a place where there is no injustice, pain, despair, depression, or despondency. In the kingdom there is no poverty, no crying, no abuse; there is no selfishness, anger, lust, or greed. It's a place of perfect peace, rest, community, joy, meaning, and relationship with the Triune God.

Jesus modeled kingdom life, and he gently bids passersby to trade in their self-oriented, fear-based existence for the fresh air of freedom, power, creativity, beauty, influence, simplicity, and love. And he allows any person who wants it the deepest privilege of helping heaven touch down on planet Earth. That's what this book is about.

May the message of the gospel—and most importantly, its life—find its home in your heart and its heart in your home.

INTRODUCTION

A Tiny Portal into a New Jesus

It was the twelve-day trip of a lifetime. I joined a fifteen-person band of would-be ambassadors of reconciliation to the Middle East, a place that 95 percent of us are tired of hearing about because we suffer from "terrorism overload." All we hear about from this area is incessant fighting over religion, politics, and that sandy and mountainous piece of real estate everyone calls their "Holy Land."

What I experienced was mind-blowing.

The trip began in southern Beirut, Shiite Muslim territory. A year earlier we had been discouraged from going there, as it was perceived to be too dangerous. This time, though, we met with the number two leader of Hezbollah. And even though it was just eighteen hours before he would lead the president of Iran through the city, he sat with us for almost four hours. He shared his hopes for peace, love for our Scriptures, and respect for Jesus, and he smiled as one of our team members knelt in prayer at his feet.

I normally would have dismissed this man's behavior as a propaganda show. But we were relative nobodies, we didn't bring an entourage of news media, and all we wanted was to gather information about his thoughts on Jesus. What reason did he have to give us a show? We also met with a handful of Muslim national leaders who spoke passionately and lovingly about how they viewed Jesus based on reading the Qur'an.

From there we moved into the land of all lands. The first two nights were spent in the little town of Bethlehem. I had expected to find beautiful Christmas lights and soft-hearted shepherds guarding their sheep by night. Instead we found a traumatized town of forty thousand people who couldn't travel to the next neighborhood because a thirty-foot cement wall and barbed wire held them inside. The majority were anti-Israel Palestinians. Looking at their living conditions, I could see why they were anti-Israel. I wondered why I rarely heard their side of the story on the nightly news and from Christian news reports. The Palestinian Christians I met in Bethlehem had as vibrant a faith as I'd ever seen.

The next day we headed to Jerusalem. Being near the place where Jesus actually kicked up dust was humbling. Once we got in the van, I didn't want to talk to anyone. I just wanted to look out the window and see the places I had read about and only dreamed of seeing. The thought of experiencing the actual places where Jesus walked and talked was almost too much for my mind to take in.

As we approached the walled city, our guide took us to the eastern side of Jerusalem to the top of the Mount of Olives and the Garden of Gethsemane. Anticipating that we would get to stroll through groves of olive trees and perhaps retrace the paths where Jesus cried, sweat blood, and agonized with his friends over the coming horror of the cross, I readied my heart for a spiritual highpoint. Instead, all we saw was a hillside of gravestones. Jewish graves cover the landscape because Jews believe the Messiah will come from the clouds over the eastern wall, and they want their dead to be the first to rise. A few small olive bushes sprinkled the hill, but it looked more like an urban junkyard than the place where Jesus walked. A letdown to the max!

Eventually we made it inside the walls of the Old City. And like a child who finally got to Disneyland only to find an empty parking lot, my last hope of imagining Jesus in this place was dashed. All I could see were more walls, modern-day money-changing concession stands, and churches from a dozen old-line denominations erected as territorial monuments. Muslims, Roman Catholics, Greek Orthodox, Armenian Orthodox, Syrian Orthodox, Coptic Orthodox, Ethiopian Orthodox, and a number of Protestants had all dug in their outposts here. Everything was stones, signs, and churches.

I tried to find Jesus, I really did. I headed toward the Wailing Wall but was yelled at by two arm-waving, toothless Hasidic Jewish cops for not putting on a head covering before I entered the Jewish zone. We walked the Via Dolorosa where Jesus carried his cross, but we got caught in a maze of people and then bombarded by shops and vendors selling everything from Nike tennis shoes to ornate hookah pipes. A few Franciscan tour guides let people take turns carrying plywood crosses through the corridors, but instead of weeping at the place of Christ's brutal last walk, I dropped a few shekels and bought an ice cream cone.

By that point I was pretty much done. Resigned to the fact that we would never actually see anything Jesus-ish, we rolled our eyes and took the last tour through the Church of the Holy Sepulcher—the place believed to be the site of Golgotha and Jesus's tomb. The Church of the Holy Sepulcher was buzzing with tourists and the background noise of multiple church services all competing for the adoration of onlookers. I felt like I was back in high school listening to two cheerleading squads yelling at each other: "We've got spirit, yes we do! We've got spirit, how 'bout you?"

Stepping down the staircase that would lead us to the tomb of Jesus, we were told to follow our tour guide. He was going to take us to a display of what they think was the real tomb. Turning the corner, I saw one of our team leaders whisper and draw a few of us aside. "Hey . . . come here . . . I want to show you a place you can really see the tomb." Four of us followed him, and being the last one to enter a small catacomb behind the actual tour, I saw some of our team looking through a little crack in an iron door. They looked excited, and I desperately wanted to see too, but our tour guide caught us and pressured us to rejoin the tour. Fortunately, on our way back, I saw the dark hallway that led to the spot and decided to make a break for it. I ducked under the low ceiling and had a few seconds all to myself. At first I couldn't even find the place to look through, but as I ran my fingers over the thousand-year-old iron door, I felt a small keyhole. Quickly I positioned myself low enough and was able to see what many believe to be the actual tomb of Jesus.

I was amazed. I finally had my moment with Jesus. I leaned my head against the dusty old door and stared at the small cave-like opening. My breathing slowed, and prayerfully I whispered, "Thank you for dying for me . . . thank you for . . ." But just as I was settling in for a private man-time with Jesus, a handful of priests filed in the room I was looking into, laughing and joking and drinking the rest of the communion wine they had just served. They completely blocked my view again, and my holy moment was over.

For a second I found a portal into seeing Jesus. Then it was gone. As I left the city, I was more than a bit despondent. I stared out the window and lamented my day in the holy city and how religion, religious people, pious performances, and massive stone impediments had blocked me from seeing the real deal.

In the place where Jesus spent so much time, today it is really hard to find him. I think few would disagree that in America, it's not much different.

Jesus and Bad PR

I don't want to come across as negative. I see no reason for venting just to vent. I've struggled through these feelings now for twenty years, and I have huge hope for future Jesus followers because for some odd reason, everyone still seems to like Jesus, or at least the historical persona they've heard about. Yet honesty demands that Christians be the first ones to acknowledge the dissonance and disorientation we've caused millions of people. We have derailed their efforts to find and follow him. The pain of this is real, and we must fight against anything that plugs the keyhole and keeps the real Jesus from being seen.

My pain? It comes from the Jesus images I grew up with: the co-opted white-bread suburban Jesus; the institutional pope Jesus; a Jesus who looks more like an angry, judgmental cop or an out-of-touch Alzheimer's patient. The Jesus I believe in and have always been crazy about is different from the Jesus so many around me describe and worship. And it's not always stone walls and religious vendors that keep people from seeing a glimpse of the real Jesus; it's often the layers of perception people have about Christians. In my world, when I meet someone new, I rarely say I'm a pastor. I'm always a "nonprofit consultant." Even my daughters introduce me to their friends by saying, "Hey, this is my dad. He's a pastor and has a tattoo." They just want to make sure their friends know that even though I lead a church, I'm not a complete dork. You've likely experienced this yourself as you've tried to explain to someone that you're a Christ follower. A part of us wants to help round out the bad PR about Christ with the cool stuff we love about him.

When the popular image of Jesus collides with the reality of the Jesus of Scripture, it can be a little shocking, even disorienting. As someone who cares deeply about people outside the Christian faith, I find it sad that the first thing I have to do to help them keep moving toward the God they're looking for is apologize for what they've run into so far. As a pastor, I lament that a high percentage of those inside the church have lost their sense of mission because of a myriad of bad Jesus images they've been force-fed for too long.

Here is a truth that affects us all: what you believe about Jesus is the most important influence in your life. You see, our beliefs affect our attitudes, our attitudes affect our behaviors, and our behaviors determine our future. Proverbs 23:7 says, "For as he thinks in his heart, so is he" (NKJV).

If a kid grows up despising his dad, then hears other people using the term "Father" in reference to Jesus, he may always have a hard time wanting to be close to God.

If someone sees Jesus as an ancient God who is "up there somewhere" watching over the bigger issues of global chaos but who is either unconcerned with our daily plight or too feeble to actually pry himself from his padded heavenly throne to lend a hand and plug the darn hole in the Gulf oil well for BP, this person may end up feeling casual about religion but have no sense of destiny, no passion to make the world better.

If Jesus is described, as he often is, as the nice son of his passive-aggressive daddy, folks tend to think of him as their buddy.

If someone's Jesus is the Clint Eastwood figure coming back to wipe out all the greasy sinners, they'll tend to take on the attitude of a mercenary and feel justified in being a butthead for Jesus, offending anyone and everyone as they literally try to scare the hell out of them.

If someone views Jesus as the head of the church but can't stand the church, they'll be stuck trying to maintain some sort of "spiritual life" without any connection to God's people.

Who was my Jesus image growing up? Well, probably the closest composite is Rex in the movie *Toy Story*. Rex is the green Tyrannosaurus rex with big teeth and a big growl but a very wimpy heart and short little arms. He represents the type of Jesus who would talk a big game but couldn't really do much to help the world other than scare us into some afterlife existence.

If you believe, consciously or subconsciously, that Jesus is any of these caricatures, your belief will be reflected in your faith and your (lack of) faith-full living. Your heart will shrivel up, your mind will turn off, and your actions will not reflect a smidgen of God's calling for your life.

I believe Jesus is a big deal—the central big deal of the faith. And if you don't have a true picture of who he was and is, you may never find the God you're looking for. And certainly you'll never tell anyone about him.

Thinking of My Daughters

They tell new writers and speakers to begin by imagining the audience you most want to reach. I'm writing this book with my two teenage daughters in mind. Every parent wants their kids to know what they think are the keys to life, their values, goals they might have set, and stories that are important to them. I want this book to show my girls what their dad thinks about Jesus. Yes, I realize they may be fifty years old before they are interested in reading their ol' dad's opinions on the meaning of life and God. Since right now they don't even want my opinion on which blouse to wear (turtleneck always, even in summer), I want to write these thoughts down before I am too old to remember where I put my teeth. In fact, let me just pause right here and write to my daughters directly:

Dear Alli and McKenna,
As I write this you're sixteen and fifteen, and you know your dad isn't exactly a normal pastor guy. Throughout my life I've always had a deep love for Jesus. But more often than not I've struggled with my role as a professional God guy. I've struggled with the church, Christians, organized religion, and of course my own failures to live the life of a real Jesus follower.

25

My faith began in the fourth grade, and I'll never forget the moment Jesus made sense to me. In the fifth grade I sold marijuana out of my trombone case, but I also memorized the books of the Bible, which earned me my first concordance from my Sunday school teacher. By eighth grade I was completely turned off by Christian friends, but at the same time I really wanted my other friends to find God. From that time all the way through high school, I quit going to youth group but had deep times of prayer with Jesus about many family issues. And, oddly enough, I felt a call to ministry.

In college I was the go-to guy for the spiritually curious or the suicidal students, but I was losing my interest in church. While at seminary I got kicked out of a few classes simply for asking questions that challenged the professors' iron-clad theology.

Then came ministry—one church in Portland, then the second in Denver. Each time the church I helped lead became a place where the spiritually disoriented found a safe place to belong. Yet each time I got into a good amount of hot water with Christians. Some got mad because I was nice to gay people; some thought I shouldn't hug young girls who were prostitutes, even though they were in our church; some thought I was a bad leader because I had a beer with some normal blokes along the way or because I didn't preach the way they thought I should.

Don't get me wrong. I feel like the luckiest man in the world because so many Christ followers have been the most inspirational, salt of the earth people I'm proud to call my friends. But I just want you to know that every day has been a fight to hold out, figure out, and dig out the real Jesus for myself and others.

I hope that as you read this, you'll find the Jesus I did and that you'll let him pull you into a future so amazing, you could never dream it up on your own. I hope you'll never be religious, conservative, liberal, or concerned about what anyone thinks of you but only be what the real Jesus of the Bible calls you to be. And then I hope you'll find like-minded and like-hearted friends who fight to live like Jesus together. And I hope you call that "church."

If you find the real Jesus, you'll really love him. Jesus challenged and deconstructed religion. He brought people together. He helped people with their practical needs. He fought evil. He changed hearts.

He was the exact representation of God, so if you ever want to know what God is really like and what his hopes for humanity are, all you have to do is find the real Jesus.

Love,
Dad

Okay, maybe you felt a little awkward listening to me talk to my girls, but I hope it gives you an idea of my heart for anyone who reads this. I simply want to help you find the keyhole and give you a chance to see Jesus without all the goofy stuff blocking your view.

Let's go.

SACRILEGIOUS JESUS

Breaking Images for the First and Last Time

On Christmas Eve I went to St. Patrick's Cathedral. . . . It had dawned on me before, but it really sank in: the Christmas story. The idea that God, if there is a force of Love and Logic in the universe, that it would seek to explain itself is amazing enough. That it would seek to explain itself and describe itself by becoming a child born in straw poverty . . . I just thought: "Wow!" Just the poetry. Unknowable love, unknowable power, describes itself as the most vulnerable. There it was. I was sitting there, and . . . tears came down my face, and I saw the genius of this, utter genius of picking a particular point in time and deciding to turn on this. Because that's exactly what we were talking about earlier: love needs to find form, intimacy needs to be whispered.

To me, it makes sense. It's actually logical. It's pure logic. Essence has to manifest itself. It's inevitable. Love has to become an action or something concrete. It would have to happen. There must be an incarnation. Love must be made flesh.

Bono[1]

I have to give you a warning before I share the following story. Some will yell "Sacrilege!" and close the book, too offended to read on. But I implore you to suspend judgment. This story took place in my own backyard. It was the starting place for this book. It motivated me to write about the difference between the real Jesus and the sanitized Jesus of religious tradition.

About eight years ago we were in our first year of starting a church. A gal next door was very close to our family and offered to help in any way she could. She wasn't a Christ follower, but she had a huge heart for people and for us personally as friends. She became very involved in our children's ministry, but her husband, "Big Billy," was not fond of me, God, or anything that resembled the traditional church world in which he grew up in inner-city St. Louis.

What I knew of Billy was that he beat up my neighbor in a fight, got shot through the eye by his friend while out hunting and walked out of the woods to live another day, and left St. Louis because of his mafia/gang connections. I wasn't sure whether that last one was fact or legend, but suffice it to say, Billy was one tough hombre.

One day while mowing my backyard, I looked up and saw Billy standing on his deck waving to me. As my eyes focused, I realized he was actually flipping me off. You know, giving me the bird. I didn't quite know what to do, so I just gave him one of those head nods, hoping to communicate, *I see you, buddy, but I am ignoring your finger*. I made one more pass with the mower and looked up again, hoping he'd be gone, but there he stood, like a statue, his finger saluting in my direction. Was he kidding? Was he serious? What did he think I would do?

I've been in many interesting situations, so this didn't seem as strange as you might suppose. But I do remember thinking, *Now, hmm, what would Jesus do?* (This was before the WWJD craze.) I have always been intrigued by how people find faith in God, and I try to be playful in situations like this. I could have been more textbook, I suppose, but in all my seminary studies I don't remember a chapter on how a Christian leader should handle the bird.

Nevertheless, I figured I'd best make a decision fast since one more pass by him without a response would communicate I was (a) afraid of him or (b) offended. Neither response was what I thought Jesus would do. A quick prayer and some deep theological analysis brought me to the conclusion that I needed to alter the playing field a bit—you know, do something this guy wouldn't expect from a pastor, or a "vicar," as he called me once. (I initially thought *vicar* was a derogatory swear word, but come to find out, it means "priest in training.")

So on my next pass, I parked the mower right next to the fence where Captain Hook was standing and let go of the handle, which shut down the motor, creating an awkward silence. As the robins peacefully chirped in the background, I reached back into the archives of my adolescence and lifted both hands high into the air, responding to tough Billy with the "double bird." That's right, the pastor one-upped him. Two birds for one stoner! I didn't just give him the double bird; I held my hands up and stared at him with a kind of Clint Eastwood glare. But even while glaring, I couldn't help picturing Big Billy jumping over the fence and beating me over the head with my own mower, St. Louis mafia style.

To my great surprise, Big Billy slowly cracked a smile and started laughing. "F—, you wanna drink?" he asked.

From that moment on Billy became my neighbor.

31

Fast-forward. It may sound like a fairy tale ending to *Godfather IV*, but I swear it's true. Billy's family became a part of our faith community, and they are dear friends to this day.

Defining *Sacrilege*

Now is a good time to define *sacrilege* or *sacrilegious* as I'll be using the terms in this book. To commit sacrilege is to *de-sacredize* what is deemed to be sacred. Sacred is defined as "consecrated to or belonging to a god or deity, holy." In the Christian sense, to commit sacrilege means to disregard, disrespect, or be irreverent toward those things that have traditionally been considered holy, venerated, or dedicated as sacred. It's tipping holy cows.

At face value this may sound bad, wrong, disrespectful, and insensitive, like Roseanne Barr butchering "The Star-Spangled Banner." In actuality, as I'll show, de-sacredizing what *should* be de-sacredized is not only good, it begins to move us toward the undercurrent of the *real person* and Good News of Jesus. Sacrilege is about removing religion from our faith. It's about securing the integrity of what is most important. It's about chipping away at people's false assumptions about who Jesus is and what following him is all about.

In truth, when done correctly, sacrilege will allow you to relax spiritually, exhale, and begin to come alive, becoming more real in your faith and in your way of being with others.

I'm not interested in controversy for its own sake. I have never enjoyed theological debate, but I can't help but speak passionately about the kind of truth that really sets ordinary men free, like it did me. I will not ask you to be profane, to desecrate, or to defile. These three words refer to a deliberate attempt to belittle, hurt, or dehumanize someone or their beliefs. Such sentiments are often steeped in angry rebellion or adolescent arrogance. They are tantamount to trashing, abusing, polluting, or destroying those things that are *genuinely holy* and important to God and to people.

Jesus did none of this. He was, however, without question, the most appropriately sacrilegious revolutionary of all time, and his call for anyone who follows is to be like him.

The world needs a tidal wave of sacrilegious apprentices.

Jesus the Iconoclast

Jesus was the true iconoclast. *Icon* means image or idol. *Clast* means to break. Every word Jesus said and act he did smashed the spiritual, religious, traditional, and pop idols of his day. False kingdoms were exposed, false motives were laid open, false teachings were confronted, and every person he touched came away confused, intrigued, perplexed, or changed. He was not liked by everyone, but he was loved by the right people—the people with eyes to see and ears to hear fresh truth.

Whether he was challenging people's view of Scripture, hanging with prostitutes and half-breeds, letting his disciples eat without ceremonially washing their hands, providing wine to guests of a wedding bash who had already partied too much, or touching lepers, Jesus went against almost every religious norm and won the hearts of the heathen. His ability to de-sacredize the sacred (when doing so was important to the purposes of God) magnetized people to him, and his followers were expected and empowered to do the same.

The real Jesus was the ultimate sacrilegious leader. Therefore, adopting a sacrilegious approach to faith may be just what the doctor ordered, particularly in a world that is ailing to see a real Jesus again. Just as Jesus turned over the junk in the temple (see Matt. 21:12–13), so we have to begin turning over the junk of our religious training. We need to get to the purity of the gospel again. This book is about recovering, or maybe discovering for the first time, the Jesus you'd naturally and sincerely want to follow and invite others to follow as well.

When we picture people converting to Christianity, we probably envision a doctrine-heavy preacher imploring people to respond to the spoken word, walk the aisle to the altar, and receive Christ into their hearts. Although this is an experience many of us hold dear in our own conversion story, we must realize that the first people that followed Jesus weren't following doctrine, theology, or the spoken word. They were following the incarnate Word, the man, Jesus the person. They didn't know anything about the cross, sin, the need for a substitutionary payment, or all the doctrine we've added on since he lived among us. They started with him alone and learned the rest along the way.

Jesus the Likable

Remember this key piece of historical truth: common people loved Jesus! What's more, they liked him.

One day while I was driving with my daughter McKenna, she said, "Dad, I love you." I reached over and clutched her leg, as I always do. Then I heard even better words: "I also like you a lot." Most parents would give their left thumbnail to have their kids respect, revere, and honor them. Nothing's wrong with that, but there's something even better: their desire to be with you and possibly to be a little like you.

If you let it, that's where sacrilege is going to take you.

People revered Jesus back then, and many still do today. No, not everyone, but some pretty significant masses still think he's the most inspiring man to have walked the earth. We have to remember that back in Jesus's time, before they really knew who he was and what he was doing in the world, the average Jacob and Martha *liked* Jesus. Similar to when you meet a person you click with at a party, they were amazed at his accessibility and his acceptance of everyone. Notice that the people who did not like Jesus—the Pharisees, for example—were people in power. Common folk couldn't get enough of him, though. They were surprised by his candor, honesty, riddles, and wit. They marveled and were sometimes even intimidated by his blatant disregard for the rules and regulations of the day, although they must have secretly loved it. I often imagine the children sticking their tongues out at the disciples, who had tried to shoo them away, as they sprinted toward the open arms of Christ.

His ways would have flown in the face of many who tried to control and oppress the people through religious legalism. Yet, at the same time, they must have felt a gentle prick in their conscience when he seemed to disregard or even condemn their traditions and spiritual viewpoints. As Jesus continued to teach, he not only tipped their sacred cows—he slaughtered some.

If you could have been a contemporary embedded reporter getting on-the-ground quotes from those who were following Jesus, you might have heard (Americanized) statements like these:

"Did you see the look on those punk Pharisees who were getting ready to chuck a rock at that whore when Jesus stepped in and made them back down?"

"Wasn't it awesome that he was willing to heal Claudio and Melpis on the Sabbath?"

"Can you believe he picked Peter, Andrew, and John to be his students? Heck, they're just fishermen. You don't have to have many credentials to get in good with this guy, eh?"

"Don't you think it's kind of weird that Jesus spends so much time with women, especially that Mary chick? I wonder if his motives are as pure as he claims."

"Have you recovered from the wedding feast this week? Sheesh, I was pretty done, but when Jesus made more wine, I just had to keep celebrating. That was quality vino!"

"You know what's most amazing to me now that he's come back from the dead? I knew him when he was twenty-one, just working in his dad's shop. He never said a word about who he was. I remember a deal he gave me on the chair I bought for my mother. Great chair too!"

This is why the early followers got to the point of no return with Jesus. They were drawn to him, followed him at great cost, and spoke endearingly about his legacy on their lives. They viewed him as if he were a god—and that's exactly what he was: the one true God.

His first and earliest followers got to experience both his strange divinity and his impressive humanity. We don't. We have to read between the lines. From the time of Jesus and the apostles until now, the church has lost so much influence, especially among normal, everyday people. What happened? We have missed something—something huge.

We have blandly imagined Jesus to be a little icon of a man we hang on chains around our necks and whose image we use in stained glass windows. We salute him when we score a touchdown or hail him when we win a Grammy Award for our raunchy rap song. We put him on T-shirts and bumper stickers. We write sappy teenage pop songs that make him sound more like a groping boyfriend than the Creator of the universe. We market him; we exploit and misuse his words to browbeat, judge, and injure the world. And in the name of "discipleship," we gather every week to reread his words, often, sadly, without giving much serious thought to becoming a smidgen more like him.

It's no wonder people today have had to conclude he's just another man who happened to start a prolific religious sect. But it's time to say it: he wasn't trying to start a religion! He wasn't trying to put a church building on every corner. His highest hopes were not that millions of people would gather on Sundays to enjoy learning doctrine about his moral codes. He doesn't care if you are a Republican or a Democrat, but he does care that much of the world is turned off by millions of people who claim him as their leader.

Here's a truth I want you to pause to consider for a moment: *Jesus's ability to influence the hearts of man and woman, child and king, prostitute, peasant, and priest was greatly due to his sacrilegious ways of behaving, speaking, listening, loving, and living.*

Rich outcasts would climb trees to see him, similar to the way glassy-eyed teenagers stare at LeBron James as he enters the arena. The poor, the hungry, the broken, and those left behind found hope in him the way young African Americans found hope in Jackie Robinson, Cassius Clay, Martin Luther King Jr., and President Barack Obama. Great leaders were afraid of him, but commoners felt safe to approach. The smartest of the day were challenged by his superior wit and wisdom, while the uneducated were promoted to the highest posts and chosen to represent him and share his message and life of good news.

Being Careful with Jesus

Writing a book about Jesus is not something to do haphazardly. While not much risk is involved in writing a poorly thought-out love song, you really don't want to create some goofy image of Jesus to fit your own whims or preferences. That's called idolatry, and it doesn't sit well with the real Jesus. You also don't want to project or infer too much beyond the biblical record, for that can lead people astray or even manipulate them into all sorts of trouble. I think of Ricky Bobby and Cal in *Talladega Nights*, sitting around the table processing their preference for Baby Jesus. Christians tend to prefer their own version of Jesus. If I say something like, "I see Jesus kinda like Lynyrd Skynyrd . . ." the theological police are going to ask for a few back-up texts, and I don't blame them.

Rest assured, I do not take this subject lightly. I know whatever I write about Jesus needs to match what the Bible says. Through the centuries others have written about Jesus as the payment for our sin, the sacrificial Lamb, Creator God, the judging King, holy man, prophet, heavenly Father—all good and right. My hope, though, is to present a biblical Jesus who models how to relate to normal, real people. How did he interact with men, women, and children? What can we learn from his example? And most importantly, how can we pattern our lives after his?

Hitting the Reset Button

Journey with me, then, back to the time of Christ. People were spiritual, just like today, and also confused, yes, just like today. The Jews had not heard from God through any prophets for more than three hundred years. In despair, they had settled back into systems of religion, the legalistic faith of the Old Testament law given to Moses. In a sense they had forgotten this huge, personal story that had unfolded between them and God, a story that was meant to bring blessing to the whole world, and now were just going through the motions of sin management and church (or synagogue, as they called it).

The non-Jewish subcultures of the Greeks and Romans believed in an impersonal force that hung in the clouds and somewhat directed human affairs. They called this higher power the Word or Logos.

In both cases, people held the view that God was distant. In the Jewish culture, they'd moved away from walking and talking in relationship with God into a system of rules and regulations. In Greek and Roman culture, they just saw God (or gods) as a distant power monger to be pleased and appeased.

It was this spiritually disoriented world that Jesus entered with a radical message and even more radical life. John writes, "So the Word became human and made his home among us. He was full of unfailing love and faithfulness. And we have seen his glory, the glory of the Father's one and only Son" (John 1:14 NLT).

The Message paraphrase says it this way: "The Word became flesh and blood, and moved into the neighborhood. We saw the glory with our own eyes, the one-of-a-kind glory, like Father, like Son, generous inside and out, true from start to finish."

And the NIV says it in the most literal way, "The Word became flesh and made his dwelling among us. We have seen his glory, the glory of the one and only Son, who came from the Father, full of grace and truth."

Frankly, our world is just as spiritually disoriented as it was in the time of the first incarnation of Jesus. Just substitute "American Westernized Christianity" for "Jews who'd turned a relationship into rules" and our spiritual-but-not-religious population for the Greek and Roman philosophies, and everything old is here again. Incarnation means to "take on flesh." It's the most profound idea of the Christian faith—that the impersonal Word became personal, that theology and doctrine came in the form of fleshy humanity—and it was God's only way to cut through the bull of religion and nebulous spirituality so that we could get a handle on a truer image of God.

As I stated earlier, what you believe about who Jesus is will be the most important thing affecting who you become, what you do, and how much you experience the living God. As God incarnate becomes fleshy—"alive"—to you, you will likewise become more fleshy to the world.

Sacrilegious Jesus . . . How about sacrilegious *you*?

To consider: What is your image of Jesus? Write down your honest thoughts about how you view him. Where did you pick up these images?

 To do: Begin drafting a letter to your children or friends about your heart for them to know the real Jesus. We will revisit this at the end of the book, so begin writing a short history of your faith journey to this point.

"If I am not allowed to laugh in heaven, I don't want to go there."

Martin Luther

2

WHY JESUS DOESN'T WANT
ANY MORE FOLLOWERS

From Disciple to Apprentice

In the 1870s the emperor of Japan waged civil war against an ancient sect of Japanese warriors called the samurai. Japan was caught between the emperor's desire to open free trade with the Western world and the samurai's concern about losing the customs and culture of the revered Japanese way of life. As portrayed in the fictional film *The Last Samurai*, the emperor hired an American military man, Captain Nathan Algren, to teach his army modern warfare techniques. Algren eventually got captured by the samurai and ended up becoming not only a student of but also an advocate for the way of the samurai. Following are a couple of excerpts from his journal:

Spring 1877: *"They are an intriguing people. From the moment they wake they devote themselves to the perfection of whatever they pursue. I have never seen such discipline. I am surprised to learn that the word Samurai means, 'to serve,' and that Katsumoto believes his rebellion to be in the service of the Emperor."*

Winter 1877: *"What does it mean to be Samurai? To devote yourself utterly to a set of moral principles. To seek a stillness of your mind. And to master the way of the sword."*

I told you that story without telling you that Tom Cruise plays Captain Algren primarily because I'm embarrassed to say that I really liked Tom in that movie. (It's sort of like admitting that I once liked Rick Springfield, the Bee Gees, and George Michael. Sorry.)

Anyway, what I love about this movie is how it portrays someone taking on a completely new paradigm of thinking. In essence the film's theme is a perfect metaphor for what it means to be a true disciple.

As I watched this film for the first time, I couldn't help but think how the meaning of the term "Christian" has been so watered down. For many, "Christian" is a label that describes someone's general belief system. But to the first people who were called Christians and to those who actually gave them the title (most of whom were not Christian), the term was associated with a specific way of life. People knew the name meant change, transformation, and a willingness to take on a radically new way of being in the world.

In *The Last Samurai*, Algren was forced to stay through the winter of 1877 in a Japanese compound. Curious and impressed by the samurai's character and commitments, their devotion and depth, Algren eventually tried their ways, and in the end he became like the samurai, the people whose ways he was hired to eradicate.

Obviously we are not forced against our will by God to become like him, but the shift of perspective Algren underwent is instructive. We too need a shift in perspective, but not just that. We need a shift in practice. Like Algren, we need to be overcome by a whole new way of living and being.

And therein is the hope of this book. I don't want to guilt you into more religion, more fervency, or more church. My aim is to expose and explore a new way of life with God that is so attractive, you will literally wake up every day looking for ways to live like your sensei, Jesus. (*Sensei* means *servant*, so it seemed like an apt term.) I want to inspire and help you imagine a life completely re-formed after the incredible life of God's chosen One.

Along the way we'll have to expose many of the false assumptions, not to mention the poor results, of contemporary, church-focused Christianity. (By the way, "church" is only mentioned a few times in the New Testament, whereas "the kingdom of God" is mentioned over 150 times.) By the end of this book, you'll see my love for the church, and I hope a fresh look at Jesus will help you renew your vision for church, as well as everything else.

If you are considering the predominant paradigm of Christianity, I hope to persuade you away from it. Not away from the central message of the gospel or Jesus; just away from what has become the religion around Christianity. If you've been a Christian for a decade or two, I hope this book will prompt you to ask whether you're really satisfied with the spiritual status quo. My guess is you've been looking for more for a long time.

To get started, let's take a look at the idea of being a "disciple" as we know it today.

Thinning the Crowd

As we get started, the first thing you need to know about Jesus is that he isn't into having a ton of adoring fans. Early in the Gospels, we see multitudes of people following Jesus. Some heard about how he was healing; some liked his teaching; some were desperate for a handout; and some were looking for a political leader. Each had their own reasons for being a part of the crowd. If Jesus was going to plan a global takeover and start a new religion, you'd think he would be thrilled to have so much street buzz. Anyone clamoring after you with applause and adoration is a plus; as long as they are out there making noise for you, it's all good. Right?

Wrong. In fact, as Jesus's followership increased, oddly enough, he intentionally began to thin the crowd. We'll delve into the details of how and why he did this later, but suffice it to say, Jesus apparently did not feel the same pressure most pastors feel. He did not pander to the individualistic desires of his fan club, he did not try to bait and switch people, and he most certainly did not model a "seeker-sensitive" approach to changing the world. Jesus was honest because his goals were simple. He wanted people to become like him: sacrilegious, incarnational people who lived a contagiously countercultural, kingdom-centered life. How have most people missed the issue of disciple making when we've preached millions of sermons and written thousands of books on discipleship? My guess is we have not become disciples because we were discipled by *followers*. Confused? Let me say it another way: followership, instead of true discipleship, has been the norm, and thus we Christians have produced a lot more people who are like *us* than people who are like *Jesus*. Somewhere along the way the original meaning of discipleship was lost.

At one time Christ followers lived every moment in the teachings and style of their leader. But somewhere along the way these adventurers turned into adherents of doctrine. People of faith became risk-averse. Kingdom revolutionaries succumbed to the world's kingdoms. Counterculture architects became wards of the state, sellouts, and seeker-sensitive consumers.

Everyone follows someone. Although we like to think we are individuals, in truth we are mostly the sum of our influences. We're the sum of the conflicts we've had, the warm experiences we've known, the graves we've knelt at, the books we've read, and the people with whom we're connected.

We are each of us a unique amalgamation of our influences, some we've adopted and perhaps some we've rebelled against. Following is a list of statements that represent the environment of my Western evangelical upbringing. Many of these ideas were "caught" rather than "taught," meaning they represent propositions that were embodied in what Christians around me actually did, rather than what they may have said:

- Western ways of doing things are intrinsically superior to Eastern ways.
- Truth is ultimately a body of propositions rather than a Person—a doctrinal download that we are to download to others.
- It is wise to invest my money in financially prospering neighborhoods because I will get the best return on my money, rather than investing in a poor neighborhood where the return might be eternal but not monetary.
- The kingdom is in the afterlife, so there's no need to help folks on this side of eternity. What matters is whether we get them into "the kingdom," another word for "heaven."
- Jesus prefers me to spend most of my time with other Christians.
- The best investment of time and energy in relationships should be determined by what I'll get in return.
- My family should have the best of everything, and I define "best" as life in a safe neighborhood with good schools and where government and social services work well.
- My job as a parent is to protect my kids, avoid anything that could hurt them, and pray that they will always stay

in church. Never mind preparing them to live a life of sacrificial mission in the wider culture.

- Stewardship is giving God 10 percent of my money after taxes instead of seeing everything as truly his, to be used for his purposes.
- An increase in my income is a way to enjoy a better lifestyle, not a way to bless more people.
- Planning for retirement means laying aside enough money to ensure that I can maintain the lifestyle I am used to and comfortable with.
- Holiness is defined in terms of what I don't do instead of how much I act like Jesus did, with the kind of people Jesus loved. Holiness is separating me and my friends and family from the dark and dirty world.
- The Good News is a message I should communicate verbally. Good deeds are for those liberal churches. My job is to get the message out, and if people don't respond, they'll sadly burn in hell.
- Salvation is only for those who have prayed the right prayer of repentance to God.
- Discipleship is growing in head knowledge about God and not doing any of the "biggie" sins.
- My relationship with God is "personal," with very little emphasis on faith in the context of a committed community.

Sound familiar? Maybe we have some issues in common. Confusing, antibiblical messages and behavioral patterns have rubbed off on us all. These patterns don't develop in a vacuum. They form by group consensus through family, school, and church; over the lunch table at your workplace; or from what you watch or listen to via the internet and other forms of media. Unfortunately, most of us are more like our culture than we are like our unique and masterful sensei!

Am I a Follower or Disciple?

Like many, I concluded that to be a disciple of Jesus, I had to start over. I had to become like Tom Cruise at the beginning of *The Last Samurai*. I had to get bonked over the head and left unconscious, then wake up in pain and slowly start to be drawn into the curious but awkward way of this strange man Jesus. I say *man*, because I don't think Jesus expects me to strive to become God. I believe he wants me to become like he was as a human. That sounds a bit easier and more doable to me.

Some people have told me, "I get your point, Hugh, but actually, I don't think I'm just a follower. I'm pretty fired up about God and think I may actually be a disciple. For sure, I'm a good Christian."

How do they know? They check a list like the one below and measure themselves against it:

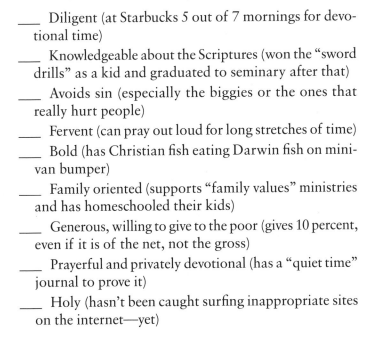

____ Diligent (at Starbucks 5 out of 7 mornings for devotional time)

____ Knowledgeable about the Scriptures (won the "sword drills" as a kid and graduated to seminary after that)

____ Avoids sin (especially the biggies or the ones that really hurt people)

____ Fervent (can pray out loud for long stretches of time)

____ Bold (has Christian fish eating Darwin fish on minivan bumper)

____ Family oriented (supports "family values" ministries and has homeschooled their kids)

____ Generous, willing to give to the poor (gives 10 percent, even if it is of the net, not the gross)

____ Prayerful and privately devotional (has a "quiet time" journal to prove it)

____ Holy (hasn't been caught surfing inappropriate sites on the internet—yet)

_____ Socially concerned (has a Compassion child photo on her fridge)

_____ Upstanding in the community (isn't a felon, pays his tickets, goes to parent-teacher conferences)

_____ Loyally attends church (regardless of a fight with spouse and kids, bad sermons, or football games, "We're going to church, dang it!")

_____ Evangelistic, willing to share the faith (looks forward to inviting friends to the Easter egg hunt, Christmas cantata, and anti-Halloween harvest party)

Not a bad list, eh? I've checked off several of these myself through the years. Truth be told, most pastors would give up their salary and one of their children if they could get one quarter of their parishioners to embody these qualities.

Well, before you pat yourself on the back, note that these and other qualities are almost exactly those of the Pharisees. Wrought with legalism, the Pharisees could have made the elder board in most US churches. Great behavior, few scandals . . . what more would any good pastor want? Ironic, isn't it, that it was these very well-behaved religious men who ended up being a hurdle rather than a bridge to bringing others into a real relationship with God?

As you look at the average non-churchgoer's main reasons for avoiding organized Christianity, the three most commonly cited are:

1. fundamentalist Christians,
2. institutional Christianity, and
3. church.

What people outside our faith tell us is that our most devoted sect of followers and the institutions that produce these followers are the main reasons they don't want to follow Christ.

Hmm. Bummer. Apparently Jesus is a lot easier to like than his followers.

So what's the issue?

I think it's simple. Today's followers are not disciples of Jesus. If they were, a much higher percentage of people would be signing up to be with them, like many did with Jesus.

Not only was Jesus a straight shooter about the cost of being a Christian, but the early Christians were intimidating as well. In one wild story recorded in Acts 5, the people in the community were giving their possessions for the common good, and one couple held back. In a shocking twist, they were exposed, and both dropped dead on the spot. The word spread about this, and as you can imagine, "No one else dared join them, even though they were highly regarded by the people. Nevertheless, more and more men and women believed in the Lord and were added to their number" (vv. 13–14).

In other words, Jesus and the early faith communities lived an intentionally countercultural life without any sense of consumer-oriented fluff—and people still chose to take the leap!

No More Discipleship

Though these pages are entirely about discipleship, I have an announcement to make: this is the last time I will use that word. It has been too sullied to be meaningful. From now on, let's change the word into what it really meant to Jesus.

Apprenticeship.

Apprenticeship is not about morality, church attendance, sticking up for God, or being a Republican. It's not about getting hired or fired by Donald Trump either. And as good as these things can actually be if done for the right reasons, it won't matter if you have a "quiet time" or are committed to a small group. It isn't important what denomination you're connected to or what translation of the Bible you like. It's not about giving money, being nice, avoiding alcohol, not cussing, or how long your daily prayer list might be. It is not about your end-times theology, whether or not you believe in a second baptism, or whether your pastor preaches exegetically or topically.

Biblical apprenticeship is about three things:

1. becoming just like Jesus,
2. doing what Jesus did, and
3. doing the above with the types of people Jesus liked spending time with.

Pretty simple. What's even better is that if we redefine the idea of apprenticeship, it becomes easy to assess how we're doing.

Here's how you can know if you are actually an apprentice: people respond to you like they did to Jesus. People are drawn to you. People seek you out for help. People like you, respect you, and want to live like you live. I'm not saying every introvert will become extroverted or the socially awkward will become the life of the party. I'm suggesting that if we take on the purpose of becoming like Jesus, the people of the world whom Jesus died for will want to be our friends. That's what an apprentice will experience.

Invariably, when I've made these comments in public, someone always raises a hand and asks about people hating us "for the cause of Christ" or pointing out the Scripture where Christ is called a "stumbling block." The questions are usually guised in a rhetorical format, so what they're really asking is, "Since Jesus was a stumbling block, shouldn't we also be stumbling blocks?" To one young man I quipped back, "So what you're asking is, 'Can I make people mad since Jesus made people mad?'"

His silence said it all. As we talked more, the group came to realize, as I'm suggesting here, that Jesus—as a living, breathing, speaking, and acting human—was quite a draw.

The only point of stumbling was his call to give up everything to follow God. That, of course, will also be where we may see some resistance, but don't mistake this one fact: Jesus was The Man! If he had owned a house, it would have been the most visited on the street; people would have asked him to coach their little league team, chair the community coalition, principal their school, host their fund-raiser, or govern their city. He would have been the first one you'd call when you wanted to go out for a beer with the guys, and you would've been desperate to have him in your house if your non-Christian buddies were coming over.

If apprenticeship means becoming like Jesus, we have quite a task before us. A lot of people have assumed they are suffering persecution from others because they are Christians. In truth, they are suffering because they are being obnoxious religious jerks (to put it nicely).

No doubt apprenticeship has some real costs, and most, if they knew what it really meant, would probably opt for religion instead of the visceral, jump-in-with-both-feet kind of experience that apprenticeship is.

So we have to answer the same question Jesus put before his first apprentices. After everyone else had left, he turned to his closest friends, gazed deeply into their eyes, and leveled them with words that also begin his apprenticeship with us: "Do you want to leave, too?" (John 6:67 NCV).

This is the question we must all consider. Do we really want to go with Jesus? Do we want to move beyond our enjoyable and encouraging fuzzy connection to him to actually become like him? Do we want to trade in our seat in the audience of curious seekers for the dirty pair of jeans he wore to serve the world? Are we willing to exchange our relational network of like-minded, nondescript, "believe what I believe" followers in order to find new friends among the least of these—even the pagans and the sinners?

If so, I invite you to try your hand at Jesus.

Let's start where Jesus started.

To consider: When you think about the amount of trouble Jesus had with the fervently religious Pharisees, is it possible that you may have some of their characteristics? Would Jesus call you a Pharisee?

 To do: To help hit the restart button, consider buying a new Bible. Let's try to start over, as if we were reading Scripture for the first time to try to find out what Jesus is really like and what he really wants from us.

"Beware of being obsessed with consistency to your own convictions instead of being devoted to God. The important consistency in a saint is not to a principle but to the divine life. It is easier to be an excessive fanatic than it is to be consistently faithful, because God causes an amazing humbling of our religious conceit when we are faithful to him."

Oswald Chambers

3

INTERLUDE INTO A NEW WORLD

Seeing Jesus in 3-D

A while ago I took my family to see the movie *Avatar*. I'm not a sci-fi guy, but since so many people recommended it, I decided that maybe the kids would like it. Because of the buzz, we got there about forty-five minutes early, but after we spent thirty minutes in the popcorn line, the only seats left were in the front row. Trying to keep the mood positive, I said, "Wow, lucky us, we get the best seats in the house." Cheryl looked over at me with that "Sure, knucklehead" look. The misery quickly turned to giddy joy as the Halter clan settled in, put on our 3-D glasses, and experienced the wonder of walking through rain forests and soaring through the air. We were in awe at how different this movie experience was. We forgot about being in the front row. Until . . .

McKenna whispered, "Dad, I'm not feeling so well." Then Cheryl took off the funny glasses, and I could tell she was about to regurgitate all the popcorn she just ate. *Hmm*, I thought to myself, *I'm feeling a little queasy myself.* No one said a word. We just looked at each other, dropped all our food, grabbed our belongings, and quickly exited. Without talking, we very deliberately walked to the car, rolled down the windows, and desperately tried not to blow groceries all the way home.

Looking back on this experience, I notice two things. First, it was the absolute coolest twenty minutes I'd experienced in a long time. We enjoyed putting on the rad Buddy Holly glasses, and as each scene unfolded, I cracked up over the looks of exhilaration and absolute awe I saw on the faces of my wife and kids. The movie was so different from anything else we'd ever seen. And second, I can't get over how unsettling it can be when you experience something completely off your grid.

As we move into looking at Jesus's first formal teachings in the Sermon on the Mount, we have to realize they were similarly paradoxical for the people who listened. They were at once exhilarating and unsettling.

Eventually, a portion of these teachings became known as the Beatitudes. Many people have written about these few verses, from many different angles. One book is titled *The Be-Happy Attitudes*. Sure, we may experience a little more happiness if we apply these truths, but Jesus's goal was much more than to make people happy. His words were meant to teach us about and challenge us toward life in the kingdom.

Jacking Things Up

Jesus messed with people's paradigms. Paradigms are those frameworks of belief and behavior that become entrenched after a certain length of time. They are filters by which we judge things, lenses by which we see things, and ruts by which we live a certain way. They are what make a culture what it is. Greeks have a way of living and thinking, as do Jewish families, as do African Americans, white suburbanites, second-generation Hispanics, and the developmentally disabled.

We all have paradigms that determine what we think is true, right, wrong, and real. Paradigms are powerful, and Jesus was moments away from smashing those of his listeners.

The backdrop to the Sermon on the Mount was the buzz circulating around Jesus. Rumors filtered across the landscape: miraculous healings, demons cast out, storms quieted with a word. People began hearing this guy might be the Messiah. He might rally the troops to start a war with the Romans so Jews could regain power.

The atmosphere must have been electric.

As Jesus began the Sermon on the Mount, many in the crowd might have thought, *Oh, this is nice-sounding stuff, and it will be worth sitting through as long as he keeps the real entertainment going—healing the sick and putting wackos in their right minds.* But as he went on, they surely would have looked at each other in bewilderment.

"What do you think he meant by *that*?"

"Did he just say what I thought he said?"

Jesus utterly jacked up everything people thought about religion and God.

And he's still at it.

Starting Over

A few years ago a good friend of mine had a stroke. He is a well-known pastor, and it was the shock of all shocks to hear of his struggle. A while later I had a chance to visit him at a rehabilitation center he was staying at. As I tried to communicate with him, it was apparent his mind was back in working order. He understood all my questions and facial expressions;

he remembered everything about our friendship and my life prior to his stroke.

But one thing was completely different. My friend could no longer communicate with ease. His speech was delayed, and he fought to find every word. His right hand didn't work very well, and he shared how hard it was for him to have to relearn everything—walking, talking, everything. As we sat over burgers and beer, I tried awkwardly to finish his sentences so he wouldn't have to struggle through every word; I attempted to order for him and concentrated on reading his facial expressions. We laughed and cried. It was awkward . . . it was beautiful.

I learned to appreciate the power and struggle of starting over. In many ways, as we "start over" in reading Jesus and his message, we should not be surprised by moments of struggle as we stretch our minds to learn new ways of seeing, walking, and talking. At times it will feel awkward. But it will also be beautiful.

To really understand Jesus's ways, you may have to suspend judgment and simply try them. I promise they will make sense later, but at first you may feel like you're boxing blind—or learning to walk and talk for the first time.

Believing What We See

A few years ago, I had a memorable discussion with an attorney named Mike. During one of our conversations I asked him about the skills required to sway a jury. He shared this story about one of his cases.

"Imagine a good man gets up every morning at the same time to care for his invalid wife who is unable to care for herself. He gets her ready and then waits for the in-home care worker who comes to watch over his bride during the day. He heads out of his house every morning at 8:45 am, takes the same road to work, works hard all day, then returns home to continue caring for his wife. Day after day, month after month, year after year. One morning, however, the home care assistant gets there ten minutes early. The man realizes he has a few extra minutes, so he decides to take the scenic highway along the coast. As he enjoys the rare freedom of feeling the salty breeze wafting in his window, he peers out and thanks God for the beauty of the ocean. Then as he approaches a traffic light, he slams on the brakes so as not to run through a yellow. As he begins to slowly drive through the intersection, a young man hopped up on alcohol runs the light, crashes into the side of the man's car, and kills him."

At this point in the story, Mike asked me, "So, Hugh, how could that terrible tragedy have been avoided?"

I thought for a few seconds and replied, "Well, maybe if he had stayed with his wife until 8:45, he would not have been in the wrong place at the wrong time, or perhaps if he'd just run the yellow light or not taken a different route to work that day, he would've been fine."

"Now let me tell you another side of this story," Mike continued. "All of the first story is true, but there's more. At the same time this man was faithfully taking care of his wife, working hard, and being a good man, there was another young man who wasn't doing so well. He grew up in the home of an alcoholic father, was abused consistently, and developed quite an anger issue. He tried not to act out, but the week of this accident, things got increasingly worse at home. His father was beating his mother and threatening him, and the young man felt like he was losing control. On the morning of the accident, the teenage boy ran out of the house to avoid another clash with his father, pulled over in the high school parking lot, got drunk, and then hurried out of the parking lot to avoid going to school. With music blaring in his truck, he approached the intersection going 70 miles an hour, failed to heed the red light, and killed the man in his car."

Mike then asked again, "So how could this tragedy have been avoided?"

I said, "Well, maybe if the boy hadn't gotten drunk, it would have not happened—or actually, if his father had not been an alcoholic, the boy would not have grown up with the need to rebel or lose control. I guess there's a lot of ways this could have been avoided."

Mike shared this lesson: "You see, Hugh, in a courtroom, people see things based on preconceived beliefs. We think people simply believe what they see, but in reality, *people see what they already believe.* Thus a good attorney must learn to tell the story in a way that helps people see things differently. If I were defending the young man, I'd tell the story from his point of view; if I were defending the family of the deceased, I'd tell the story from their angle."

Because he knew this human tendency to "see what we believe," Jesus knew it was going to be challenging to help people see the world, other people, life, and God from a new point of view. So he painted a picture of the kingdom come down to earth with vivid stories, anecdotes, and radical contrasts. Then he set out from that Sermon on the Mount to show us by example how to live the kingdom life, in the flesh, here and now. Eventually he would help us to "believe what we saw."

Before we dive into the next section, I pray that you will suspend your preconceived and potentially soul-robbing beliefs, come to the Beatitudes with a beginner's mind, and let Jesus re-form not only your way of thinking and believing but also your understanding of how we are to live and influence others.

 To consider: To reorient, one must first acknowledge the disorientation they are feeling. So make a list of the top three questions or struggles with the Christian faith that have hung you up. Give God permission to speak to these as we read.

To do: If possible, put this book on your car seat and try to read only when you're in a public place: a coffee shop, pub, or park bench. I think reading while you watch real people may clarify God's voice to you.

"The golden rule for understanding spiritually is not intellect, but obedience. If a man wants scientific knowledge, intellectual curiosity is his guide; but if he wants insight into what Jesus Christ teaches, he can only get it by obedience."

Oswald Chambers

OPEN YOUR MIND,
ENTER THE KINGDOM

Becoming an Unbiased Learner

Blessed are the poor in spirit,
    for theirs is the kingdom of heaven.

Matthew 5:3

Since I turned forty a few years ago, it's become a lot harder to lose a few pounds. Some people can lose weight by taking a bath, pulling the plug, and fighting the current three times a week. For me it requires a bit more activity. Five days of cardio isn't enough, and now I have to eliminate everything from my diet other than tree bark, green things, and chicken. In the middle of my latest depressing diet, a friend suggested I try "hot yoga." He said that yoga would stretch my muscles and strengthen my core, and the heated room would both relax me and push impurities out of my system. I'm still not sure what the heck my "core" is, but since everyone seems to be talking about it, I thought I'd give the yoga a try.

As I drove to my first session, I found myself more than a little nervous. I'd just purchased my nifty yoga mat at Target, and on the way to class I called my friend to verify what I should wear. I figured some type of leotard, a tank top, and my running shoes. He suggested I forgo the spandex and wear a T-shirt and shorts. He also suggested I do the class with bare feet. That would have been fine in my twenties, but these days my feet look like they belong to a hobbit.

I got to the session early so I could check things out, then positioned myself along the back wall where I wouldn't be noticed. I secured what I thought would be the perfect hideaway spot, but incredibly, this very wall turned out to be the one from which the instructor would teach. In fact, when she walked in she invited me to help teach the class since I was where everyone was already focused. I quickly bowed out, began to reposition myself, and told her I was a rookie. "The last time I stretched was in seventh grade gym class," I deadpanned.

She shared this clever information with the whole class. Perfect. So much for flying under the radar. All eyes were now on me to provide the entertainment.

The soothing Yanni music began, which actually sort of helped. I calmed down some. The cute little instructor led us in some breathing exercises, which boosted my confidence. "I can do this type of exercise. I'm good at breathing," I quipped. Then the fun began. She walked over to the wall and hit some button that turned our nicely warm room into Dante's Inferno. In three minutes, comfort turned to panic.

After about forty-five minutes (only halfway there), we were given some free time to work on our "wall moves." Most people did headstands, some leaned against the wall in strange ways, and others did unassisted handstands. One seventy-year-old lady was doing a modified tripod thingy where she balanced her knees on her elbows. I thought if she could do that, I certainly could. I got positioned and, surprisingly, held it! The instructor noticed my success and bent down and quietly whispered, "Very nice." I was so proud, so optimistic, so . . . in trouble. No sooner had her breath wisped off my overheated neck than I began to teeter. I tried to right the ship, but it was obvious I was leaning too far forward. Normally, falling forward isn't a big deal. I do it all the time while mountain biking. All you do is put your hands down to soften the fall. But in yoga, in this position, my hands were occupied holding my face off the wood floor.

My forehead hit the wood floor with the force and sound of a bowling ball slapping against plywood! The entire class stopped to make sure I was okay. "No worries, folks. It's all good," I offered with as much composure as possible for a guy who'd just fallen on his face.

I survived, and as I was rolling up my soaking wet yoga mat at the end of class, the instructor came over and tried to encourage me to continue. As we made light of my not-so-smooth beginning, we entered into a conversation that made the ninety minutes of misery worth it. She asked me what I did for a living, so I told her I was a pastor.

"Really? That's interesting," she said, a curious look on her face.

"Why so interesting?" I asked.

"Oh, it's just that I thought you Christian people thought of yoga as evil. I saw a CNN report today about some Southern Baptist seminary president who condemned yoga and then a few other pastors who said it was demonic. No surprise—some Christians in my own family have disowned me already, so I'm sort of used to it."

"Yeah," I said, "I know a lot of Christians who take some pretty large gray areas and turn them into small black-and-white boxes, then impose those boxes on the entire world."

Her eyes widened. "So you're a pastor and you don't just write me off?"

"Of course not! Although many Christians miss this, Christianity is an Eastern faith. It's supposed to be very holistic; it's supposed to be about a process of emptying ourselves and becoming more like God. Early Christians embraced a mysterious posture of learning, humility, and the importance of staying teachable. So although I may not totally agree with some underlying philosophies, or whatever you now believe, I assume you're still trying to figure things out . . . and so am I. I try to follow God in the way of Jesus, and I don't think I'll ever become a master at it."

We talked a little more around this theme, and at the end she smiled and said, "Wow, you're the first Christian I've met who I would like to chat with again. I actually really love Jesus, but I thought I had to leave the church just because I enjoyed teaching yoga."

"Look, Megan," I said, "even if yoga was from the pit of hell, the Jesus you love actually made it pretty clear that he didn't come to condemn the world but to save it, so you can be sure he's not exactly proud of spiritual leaders who publicly condemn people or practices."

Now and Then

The world we live in is a spiritual world. In generations past the term "spiritual" was reserved for Christians, or perhaps fervent Eastern faith followers. Everyone else was considered secular. Today, most would claim some spiritual connection to God (as they view him, her, or it). Those who claim there is no God or who have no personal faith are in the minority.

Yet while you would think hard times would move people of faith to seek deeper truth in a spirit of humility, for some, arrogance wins the day. They seem to find comfort only within the framework of their individual viewpoints. This includes Christians.

Nearly all religions have at least one branch that leans toward a fundamentalist mentality. And it is on the furthest ends of these branches that we find people who blow up planes and terrorize citizens; those who move to Montana with a backseat full of weapons, the American flag, and a

Bible; and Facebook groups that pray for the death of the president.

Sadly, Christians are no more exempt from crazy sects of "brethren" than Islam is from its segments of radical terrorists.

A question I'm asked most often when I speak about engaging in conversation with those outside our faith is, "How do I stay true to myself without belittling or judging others about what they believe or don't believe?" This question is usually followed by the admission, "I'm afraid to talk about religion right now because my own beliefs are still evolving and in process."

Most people I talk with will say in one form or another, "Jesus feels right to me. I like what I know of him. But the church? Right-wing fundamentalism? Not so much." And yet they want something deeper than generic spiritual apathy. People want to believe, and they want to talk and process their evolving thoughts aloud without fear of being shut down. I've found this to be as true with New Age followers as with Christ followers. Most people, whatever their faith, would love a safe place to simply converse, explore, and share without judgment or fear.

As Jesus traveled around the Galilean countryside, he encountered people who would have self-identified as spiritual. His own tribe was the Jewish one. Jews believed they were God's chosen people—God's favorite and most beloved ethnic minority. They were steeped in the Torah (the Law), the Prophets, and wisdom books. Many had memorized massive portions of Scripture. They had grown up hearing around the family campfire all the great stories of Hebrew heroes and their journeys with God. They were confident in their knowledge, customs, and beliefs. We could probably compare their perceptions to those of the branch of fundamental evangelicalism that has a rigid system of beliefs in place, including an "infallible" test to determine who is "in" and who is "out" of heaven or who ultimately has God's favor.

In other regions, the people Jesus connected with grew up in the Greek culture. They loved the pantheon spirituality of the Greek gods. They built shrines to Aphrodite, Zeus, Venus, Hercules, and other gods of their culture. Their gods were powerful and beautiful and gave them the freedom to enjoy life and live large.

Others of his audience were Roman, probably more secular but still deeply spiritual. For them and the Greeks, the wisdom of the great philosophers and national leaders was the focus of worship and devotion.

Mixed in with these three primary cultures were exiles of Egypt and citizens of neighboring Babylonia with their own faith and philosophical systems.

This was Jesus's religious-social context, and it was among all these different spiritualities that he said, "Blessed are the poor in spirit, for theirs is the kingdom of heaven" (Matt. 5:3).

Poor in Spirit

Emmett Fox, in his commentary *The Sermon on the Mount*, gives us this definition of "poor in spirit":

> To be poor in spirit means to have emptied yourself of all desire to exercise personal self-will, and, what is just as important, to have renounced all preconceived opinions in the whole-hearted search for God. It means to be willing to set aside your present habits of thought, your present views and prejudices, your present way of life if necessary; to jettison, in fact, anything and everything that can stand in the way of your finding God.[1]

In Matthew 18:3 Jesus said it even simpler. "Truly I tell you, unless you change and become like little children, you will never enter the kingdom of heaven."

The Greek word for poor is *protos*, and it means to be completely empty and dependent upon someone else for provision.

Think of a homeless man slumped over in abject poverty, begging for help. This is the picture of how Jesus wants his people to be. It's doubtful many of us have ever been totally without food or shelter. Sure, most of us have had some tight financial times; perhaps we have had to ask a friend or a family member for help. Even more folks have been in a credit jam and had to ask creditors for alternative payment options. In this most recent recession, hundreds of thousands were forced to file for bankruptcy or lost the mortgage on their house and had to live in a rented apartment or with relatives. So you may have "no phone, no pool, no pets," but you've got a place to lay your head with a roof over it and something, even if it is ramen noodles, to put in your stomach.

Almost all of us are rich compared to the sort of "poor" referred to in this verse. This type of poverty claims to have nothing. No collateral, no ability to earn what's needed, and no way to pay back what has been given—broke. To be bankrupt of spirit is to embody an attitude that says, "You know what? God and this thing called faith are so beyond my grasp that I am empty of the ability to know absolute truth. I know absolute truth exists. But I also know I'm a human of very small brain compared to God, and I have no problem admitting I may be wrong about many things and you may be right. Only God himself knows it all."

Said another way, "Blessed are those who don't think they have cornered the market on spiritual truth." Or "Blessed are those who stay as teachable as a five-year-old in kindergarten." This message would have sounded scandalous and contradictory to everything the spiritual philosophers of that day knew. Theirs was a world of proudly debating and striving to win the fight over words and ideas. To show humility—to be "poor in spirit"—would have been like admitting they could be . . . *gulp* . . . wrong. And possibly wrong about . . . *double gulp* . . . everything.

Unlike the philosophers of the day, Jesus did not seem interested in arguing fine points of theology or philosophy. Yes, he could give a young and brash Pharisee a theological wedgie if he wanted, but he was primarily trying to prepare his young apprentices for an entirely new paradigm of living under a new order he called the "kingdom of God." Jesus knew that any paradigm shift is difficult to adopt, especially for those who have closed their minds and want to stay comfortably stuck with what is familiar. So it's probably no surprise that he preferred being around the spiritually hungry and disoriented over the already hyperspiritual (but also hyperapathetic). Those who know it all have no room to receive radical, life-changing Good News.

When we hear Jesus say things like, "The kingdom of God has come near. Repent and believe the good news!" (Mark 1:15), we tend to think he is speaking to people outside the faith. We might find ourselves thinking, "Preach it, Jesus. And while you are at it, really lay it on those foggy followers of Eastern faiths, those yoga instructors, the Mormons, Islamic extremists, and that half-baked but ever-smiling Dalai Lama." This admonition, however, was aimed squarely at the religious conservatives of his day.

Jesus's call to repentance, if given today, would likely be to pastors, ultra-right-wing fundies, mainline and liberal traditionalists, progressive charismatics, and anyone else who believes they have things figured out spiritually, doctrinally, or theologically.

Maybe he would call you to repentance.

And me.

Yikes.

"Truth"

"Yeah, but Hugh, we have the truth now. It's the Bible. We know more than those religious leaders knew, and we shouldn't apologize for that. We can know truth, and we should make sure that the world knows the truth, don't you think?"

Yes, we do have more doctrine compiled in a nice, neat package for us, and I have no desire to dissuade anyone from clear doctrine about Christ, humanity's condition apart from God, the need for a Savior, the pure payment for our sin by Jesus on the cross, and his resurrection. These truths are central, and no matter how you read the story in its entirety or pull it apart in small sections, these facts are immovably consistent in Scripture. They are what everything else in our faith hangs upon. So yes, be confident in these things. But recognize that added to this simple message of Good News is a mountain-sized pile of dogma and questionable theology that has resulted in some truly odd practices and that waft of unconscious arrogance and judgment that people sniff out and are repelled by.

Our pet views of truth have caused the majority of church splits and the resulting hundreds of denominations. In the name of skewed or slightly skewed versions of truth, many have given themselves permission to be obnoxious at best, abusive at worst. There's the dad who forces his faith on his kids and abandons the relationship if they don't salute everything he personally believes; there's the street preacher who yells to complete strangers over a loudspeaker or stands on a street corner to spew condemnation (so he can feel he's been "persecuted for righteousness' sake"); there's the pastor who claims the right to the congregation's money, insisting they should always give money to the church over a pressing need they may see in their world or neighborhood.

Then there's you and me. Maybe we've told people they can't drink alcohol, burn incense, or learn from other religions. Maybe we've encouraged our children to have only Christian friends, avoid gays, and always go to church, because that's where God lives. Maybe our interpretation of Scripture condones our me-first suburban lives instead of calling us to address the needs of our city, the poor, and the oppressed.

This way of clinging to perceived truths, which may have nothing to do with the essentials of the gospel, creates a Grand

Canyon–sized chasm between our rhetoric about God's love and the way we actually demonstrate that love. Our perceived ideas or interpretations of "truth" have started religious wars. "Truth" has aided and abetted the practice of slavery. "Truth" has construed private piety to be more important than taking care of orphans and widows. "Truth" has taught us to blindly support whatever Israel wants. "Truth" has casually brushed aside any thought of actually loving Muslims as a path to peace and change. In other words, under the banner of "truth," millions have missed the truth Jesus preached. In many cases simple faith and humble learning have been replaced by a mountain-sized pile of ill-begotten ideas that encourage Christians to feel like they have "arrived."

Jesus Starts Here

It is no surprise that the first "blessing" in the Beatitudes signals where Jesus wants us all to begin. He wants his followers and apprentices to start over, humble themselves, and become learners. He wants us to become like children, wide-eyed and curious, in order to enter this new kingdom mentality and all it holds for us.

Over the years Cheryl and I have wondered why our twenty-something son Ryan hasn't been healed of his epilepsy. So have a few well-meaning friends. Some took me to the passage where Jesus said, "This only comes out by prayer and fasting" (see Mark 9:29). So I tried a forty-day fast. I lost a lot of weight, but Ryan still has seizures. Others said, "It's just a matter of time because God always heals us." So we've waited. For over two decades now. One couple actually came to our house and told us that Ryan's seizures were due to him watching the children's TV show *Barney*. According to this pastor, the purple dinosaur is an idol for children that sent demonic Barney spirits to inhabit Ryan and our home. He asked if he could anoint

70

our doorposts and drive away the evil spirits so Ryan could be set free. (If you bump into me, you can ask me in person how I responded. I probably shouldn't put it in print.)

Doctrine? Dogma? Or dung? Sometimes it's hard to tell the difference.

Dallas Willard said in *The Divine Conspiracy*,

> Jesus and his words have never belonged to the categories of dogma or law and to read them as if they did is simply to miss them. They are essentially subversive ways of thinking. They reflect mystery and in an Eastern sense require some subjective thoughtfulness in light of the whole story instead of focusing on individual words or sentences. John 6:63 says, "my words are Spirit and life"—exactly opposite of law or dogma. They invade our "real world" with a reality even more real, but which requires us to thoughtfully interact with the Spirit of God instead of the letter of the law.[2]

This is so helpful. Dogma, by nature, wraps God-inspired thoughts into a box and then bids you to stop thinking. It's done; you've got it all figured out. And once you have it all figured out, your only recourse is to force the entire box on someone else without considering the particularities of his or her life.

Why are our churches dying?

Why is the influence of believers decreasing?

Why is our Christian way losing its voice and respect in this country?

The answer may be found, to start with, in our arrogance and overconfidence on many noncritical theological positions.

Last week a young woman came up to me after I had spoken and asked, "What is your stance on women in ministry?"

I said, "We like women here at Adullam. I actually married one." I thought it was funny. She didn't.

"No, I mean, can a woman be a pastor here, or teach?"

"Of course," I said.

"Well, that's what I was afraid of. Obviously this is not a biblical church."

I was a bit stunned by her response. I've taken some hits before from women who didn't think we were doing enough to champion the role of women in our fellowship, and now this woman was ticked because we didn't hand every woman a cookbook and make them put on head coverings when they came through our doors.

Over the course of six years people have left our church

- because I didn't preach the way they thought I should or sanction the type of music they like;
- because we didn't take an offering and because we give people permission to tithe to the needs of hurting people around them instead of bringing it all to the church;
- because we don't have women represented enough from the microphone, or because we have too many women in leadership;
- because we let caring non-Christian people who love kids work in our nursery;
- because we won't take a hard stance on end times theology or alcohol consumption;
- because I let my daughters pierce their noses or get a tattoo;
- because we don't make sure, through some formal process, that people are certifiably "in" before we let them take communion;
- because we let people who have been divorced counsel young married couples; and
- because I have a tattoo.

I remember a man challenging me because, as he put it, "You don't have your doctrine of the Holy Spirit locked in." Pardon me a minute while I vent here. Even the Bible says the Spirit does whatever the heck he wants to do whenever he wants to do it and is like the wind in the darn trees, coming and going as it likes. So call me crazy, but I think I'll keep my mind open on this one!

Many people don't want to be teachable or open to new paradigms. It's just easier to maintain their beliefs—without question or debate—and go find others like them. And it is this very attitude that Jesus challenges in the first Beatitude.

Obviously the call to become empty spiritually doesn't mean we should shut off our brains or avoid studying Scripture or learning doctrine. It just means we don't rush to stuff truth in a box that we then use to bludgeon others.

Absolute truth is absolute. God is truth and his Word is truth. Scripture in its original languages with no mistakes, no miscues, leaves us with no need to look elsewhere for help. There is, however, one glaring problem with absolute truth, and that is that we, being humans, have a tendency to be . . . well, human. And that means we are biased, short-sighted, and very often wrong.

I believe in the absolute truth of heaven, but I'm a little sketchy about what it will be like. I'm convinced God has left us his Holy Spirit to guide us, but I'm not always sure how to relate to his invisible power. I'm sure Jesus is coming back, but I don't know if it will be before or after the Cubs win the World Series. I'm sure there's a moment in time when our conversion is secured, when God puts our names in his Lamb's Book of Life, but I'm not willing to determine that moment for everyone. I know Christ wants us to be good Christians, but I certainly don't want to presume that they should all look and act like me!

Do you get the point?

Although the Scriptures are exactly right, we have to hold our pet interpretations of debatable truths a little more loosely, with humility.

Missing the Word

Here's a wild thought: Jesus was sacrilegious with Scripture and Scripture lovers. John 5:37–40 reads,

> You have never heard his voice nor seen his form, nor does his word dwell in you, for you do not believe the one he sent.

73

You study the Scriptures diligently because you think that in them you have eternal life. These are the very Scriptures that testify about me, yet you refuse to come to me to have life.

Later Paul even referenced the problem in Acts 17:2: "As was his custom, Paul went into the synagogue, and on three Sabbath days he reasoned with them from the Scriptures."

Very interesting, isn't it, how you can grow up your whole life studying the Word and still miss the Word, the person of Jesus? The people Paul "reasoned with" were people who met weekly to pore over Old Testament prophecies about the Messiah, but they still had to be persuaded to believe in the Messiah when he showed up in the flesh.

It's odd, but Jesus had to challenge the scholars' commitment to God's revelation before he could reveal himself to them! He was actually suggesting that they really didn't know the Scriptures, though they had memorized them. It's like the difference between having a lot of knowledge and facts about your spouse based on reading about their history versus actually looking into their eyes, appreciating them, and connecting with them body and soul. It is a little like taking a kid on a road trip to explore America, but instead of looking out the window at the wonders around him, he is intent on reading about it and looking at the pictures in his geography book.

This is a powerful insight any follower of Christ must recognize and embrace: Jesus loved the Scriptures as they witnessed to him, but his biggest fights were with those who knew the most Scripture. He had his fiercest battles getting them to put down the guidebook and look at the Word made flesh in front of their eyes.

A Litmus Test for Scripture Knowledge

At the beginning of his sermon, Jesus cuts right through the bull of religion and hammers the nail of real faith. Growth in true scriptural knowledge is seated in the heart and proven by our actions. In 1 John 2 we hear the real deal. "We know that we have come to know him if we obey his commands. Whoever says, 'I know him,' but does not do what he commands is a liar, and the truth is not in that person. But if anyone obeys his word, love for God is truly made complete in him. This is how we know we are in him: Whoever claims to live in him must live as Jesus did" (vv. 3–6).

How do you know if you really know the Scriptures? You obey them, and you become like Jesus. So let's test this out. Imagine you grew up in the church, you went to Bible school and maybe even seminary, but you don't do what the Scriptures say. For instance, the book of James tells us that pure, undefiled religion, real faith, the type of Christianity God calls the essence of our belief in action, is to look after orphans and widows. So if someone doesn't do this, then they don't really know the Scriptures. Jesus taught us to consider everyone our neighbor, to bless when cursed, to turn the other cheek when mistreated, to entertain strangers, to give sacrificially of our money until it hurts, to live by faith not by sight, and a few dozen other zingers.

Do most Christians live lives like this?

No.

Thus we don't know the Scriptures, according to Jesus and John. Here's a surprising thought to chew on: you only *know* what you *do*.

When people come into our church, many of them eventually read the book that Matt Smay and I wrote called *The Tangible Kingdom* and then ask me, "Now what?"

I usually say, "Well, did you do what we suggested yet?"

"Well, not yet, but I did read it, and I get what you were talking about. So can you help me with these other questions I have, these other areas where I need advice?"

It makes me want to say, "No, not yet. You can't go on to step two until you actually do step one." You can know a lot of concepts about a lot of spiritual stuff, but according to Jesus, you don't really understand and "know truth" until you live it out.

Consider, if you will, what would happen if the majority of Christians went back to the passage we just referenced from James and decided to live out just that mandate to look after orphans and widows. What if that one admonition was our church's "Introduction to Christianity" course? Then, imagine if once people were involved helping out a kid who needed a mentor or comforting a grieving widow as part of the new routine of their lives, then and only then would we move to Christianity 201, focusing on "Love God with all your heart and love your neighbor as yourself." Because they had already *practiced* loving a "neighbor," the *concept* of this verse would already have some shoe leather to it and mean so much more. You get the point. Jesus really doesn't care how much we know if our knowledge amounts to no change in our lifestyle.

If you're someone who believes in truth and wants people to come to the truth, your best play is to start living out what you do know, piece by piece, morsel by morsel. This is how Christ's kingdom works. It's mysteriously simple and profound. Imagine you want to be the next Julia Child or Iron Chef. You come to the Food Network executives and say, "I have studied every cookbook of every great chef, and now I'd like a TV cooking show of my own."

The panel asks, "Do you have any cooking experience?"

You answer, "Well, no. I've never *actually* boiled an egg myself or anything. But I can tell you 376 different ways to cook an egg according to my studies."

One of the execs, eyes wide with amusement, might say, "Don't tell us you know how to cook. Come back when you've created thousands of memorable dishes that thousands of people have enjoyed and raved about. Get out your skillet and start cooking." In fact, a home cook with experience in making great meals for her family is more likely to get her own show than someone with a doctorate degree in food science who has never flipped a perfect omelet.

As a pastor, I can tell you I'd much rather have a church full of hands-on, sleeves-rolled-up omelet flippers than dozens of foodies with nothing but heads full of untried recipes. Why? People in the world are hungry for real food, not recipes or philosophies about food.

In the same way, people in the world are hungry to experience a real God in action. They are not eager to listen to debates or arguments about his existence. We bring more people into the kingdom with a hot meal than a hot topic.

Personally, I don't like mysteries. I'm not the type who tries to figure out episodes of *24*; I don't like suspenseful movies where you're waiting on pins and needles hoping for a good ending. I'm a nonfiction type of guy. Discovery Channel, the Food Network, or *SportsCenter*—that's how I roll. Just give me a summary of the basic facts and let me move on.

Jesus, however, is trying to take people from a small box of religion to the place where they can open up their lives to a huge new world called the kingdom. And now I am getting to why he doesn't just tell us everything plainly. Why all the parables, the stories, the anecdotes that make you go "What?" Like all the best and wisest teachers, he wants to help us enter into the process of learning by provoking our thinking and by asking us to apply new lessons as soon as possible. I believe he wants us to enjoy the never-ending experience of relating to him, finding new treasures, and never getting bored.

Allowing for mystery keeps us teachable, for we are ever on this journey of discovering God. To be frank, most genuine spiritual sojourners I know are drawn to someone who is vulnerable about this. So what about the yoga lady? Well, our conversations have deepened, and in fact, she has invited our yoga friends to join us for lunch and coffee. I'm learning about her story, and she is very interested in mine. Condemnation? No. Friends? For sure. Saved? In God's capable hands.

The Scriptures are God's inspired, divinely breathed stories, metaphors, wisdom, and teaching about the mystery of a new kind of life under the reign of God through Jesus Christ. They are a cohesive story about God, his love, and his plan for humanity, and they are still our best resource for piecing together a framework for our lives. But they are not a cut-and-dried "how-to" manual.

I've found that approaching Scripture with an openness to learning something fresh and new, "as a child," if you will, has been foundational for helping me get closer to living in the way of Jesus. It's an odd paradox that the more we come at the Bible or God or Jesus with our minds already preprogrammed and made up, the less room we leave for the Holy Spirit to surprise us and change us.

 To consider: How might you develop a humble, teachable spirit with your children?

 To do: Ask someone from another faith system to mentor you. Make a commitment not to argue with them, just to learn.

 To do: Pick one Scripture where Jesus asks us to do something and commit to doing that one thing once a week for three months. See how well you get to "know" that Scripture.

"For the Kingdom of God belongs to those who are like these children. I tell you the truth, anyone who doesn't receive the Kingdom of God like a child will never enter it."

Mark 10:14–15 NLT

5

THE PROBLEM WITH FAMILY VALUES

Why Jesus Will Ask You to Open Your Home

Blessed are those who mourn,
    for they will be comforted.

Matthew 5:4

This past year I had a week that turned into a tough stretch of days. A family from my daughter's middle school was killed in a car accident (yes, the whole family). A dear man in our church was diagnosed with cancer. My mother passed away from dementia complications. Then driving home from our church gathering, I was diverted by a policeman around a fatal car accident that took the lives of six people. I found out later that four of them were missionaries who were heading to an overseas post in just a few days. Their six-year-old son also died.

Some days we all wish we could be little kids again and just curl up on a parent's or grandma's lap for comfort and assurance that everything will be all right. There's nothing like being comforted by someone who is skilled in the art of compassion when your safe world starts to shake and fall apart at the seams.

In our last chapter, we saw that Jesus began his Sermon on the Mount with a challenge to the crowd to rethink their preconceived way of seeing the world, God, and religion. Just as people boo and leave a speech by a political figure they don't like, many may have left the hillside for more familiar pastures after Jesus dropped his first "Blessed are . . ." But those who stayed must have been glad they did, because at points of human despair, everyone wants what Beatitude #2 promises: "Blessed are those who mourn, for they will be comforted" (Matt. 5:4).

The people listening to Jesus were deeply acquainted with hard living and tragedy. Although the crowd didn't have TV news or internet to see visual images of war, human suffering, and pain as we can on a daily basis, they saw plenty of trauma. Always looking over their shoulders for thieves, conquerors, disease, or famine, they lived without heat, air conditioning, clean or easily accessible water, medical care, government help, early disaster warning systems, insurance, or pensions. So many things we rely on to give us a feeling of safety for ourselves and our kids were absent. Fear must have been a constant companion.

Seinfeld or the Nightly News?

When Cheryl and I go see a movie together or sit down to watch TV, I always want a comedy. My kids make fun of me because I tend to leave the living room whenever there's sadness or tension on the tube. I don't like it when people get hassled by the judges or kicked off *American Idol*. I never watch the first part of *Extreme Makeover: Home Edition* because I don't like hearing about the family losing their dad to the wheat combine accident, and I always click past the sad animal shelter commercials. I, like a lot of Americans, prefer not to focus on pain. And if I have my choice, I'd rather live in the "reality light" world of *Friends*, *Seinfeld*, or even *The Biggest Loser*, because there's always a happy ending.

Mourning? I try to avoid it if at all possible. And if it cannot be avoided, I'd like to fast-forward through it straight to the comforting part with the *Happy Days* ending.

If you are at all like me, we're going to have to work hard to go where Jesus wants to take us with this Beatitude. But this may be the most revolutionary change in perspective Jesus offers. Although Westernized Christianity pulls us away from risk, confrontation, and getting gritty with real issues, Christ is going to lead us into places that will capture our emotions and reorient our entire perspective about life and why we live it.

Entering the House of Mourning

What is unique to mourning is the power it has to transform our perspective. The day I received the news of my friend's stroke, I had been struggling with some mundane issues in my own life. It was Monday morning, and I was bummed out about church stuff, stressed about hitting a writing deadline, cranky over our financial situation, and a few other normal Monday morning blues. But pondering my friend's plight and the pain his family was in overwhelmed me. I pulled over to the side of the freeway and began to weep for them. As I did, my own pressures drifted away.

The possibility that my friend could die at any minute recalibrated my perspective. I was thankful for what I had instead of lamenting the small stuff that wasn't going my way. My hope once again centered on Christ, heaven, and living to leave a legacy for my own friends and family when my time is up.

In Ecclesiastes we read the memoirs of an ancient sage who was a very strange cross between, say, Hugh Hefner and a local priest. Solomon was a man who had the ability to enjoy any fleshly or worldly pleasure, and so he did, yet he still had a genuine love for God. At the end of each hedonistic experiment he sat down and put pen to paper for the rest of the world to learn from. His words cut through our shortsighted lives: "It is better to go to a house of mourning than to go to a house of feasting, for death is the destiny of everyone; the living should take this to heart. Sorrow is better than laughter, because a sad face is good for the heart" (7:2). Then later he says, "The heart of the wise is in the house of mourning, but the heart of fools is in the house of pleasure" (7:4).

Counterintuitive, isn't it? This man, who according to God had more wisdom than almost anyone who has ever lived, is suggesting that a funeral is better than a wedding; that watching a documentary on human trafficking will do more for your soul than playing another hour on your Sony PlayStation; that leaving the party early to go see a struggling friend is the way into the incarnational life of God.

But why would we choose this? Heck, life is hard enough—who needs another downer?

With all the struggles of life and misery all around us, for self-preservation's sake, maybe we should keep our heads down and mind our own business. At least that's what our flesh will tell us. Our flesh—which is our basic ego-driven selfish nature—doesn't want to mourn and will fight all day to avoid it. This is why so many are addicted to alcohol, drugs, pornography, materialism, debt, spiritual lethargy, and apathy toward the real ways of Jesus. The flesh wants to anesthetize pain rather than feel it and move through it. This is also one of the main reasons so many leave the Christian faith or fight against it. We actually get mad or jaded or blame God because we don't like the way he allows so much evil to exist. That's our flesh saying, "I don't want to take responsibility to help, fix, or comfort others in this messy world I did not create."

Shaking Hands with the World

A few months ago a couple in their late forties began coming to Adullam, the church I helped start. I'd heard they were involved in the leadership of another church across town, but for a number of reasons they were considering making a change to Adullam. For a month or so, all they did was come in smiling, and they always had a warm handshake and kind words for our community. As I got to know them, a remarkable story emerged.

Kevin had been diagnosed with cancer and hasn't been given long to live. The doctors told him not to have physical contact with people, as it could cost him his life. Most folks would huddle up in a sanitized room, but Kevin sees the situation as an opportunity to trust Jesus . . . really trust him. Maybe Kevin has already settled the death issue; quite possibly it is just a pure gift of faith. But this man shakes hands with everyone and comes early every Sunday morning to set up, clean up, and pray over the mission of Adullam.

The living, breathing, image of the invisible God left safety, security, and glory, and in spite of what it cost him, he was absolutely bent on shaking hands with disease, pain, sin, and sinners. In the second Beatitude Jesus invites the crowd of glassy-eyed observers to consider a life of mourning; that is, a life of sensitivity to the pain of others.

During the Middle Ages, early monastic communities were known for moving in where there was pain rather than moving away from it. If there was a plague or disease ravaging a community, the church often moved out with the rest of the fearful peasants, but the monastic communities intentionally moved in. During the British missionary movement, most of the missionaries going to Africa knew they would survive only a year or two because of the prolific and consuming diseases. They went anyway. Early Moravian missionaries were known to sell themselves into slavery in order to reach slaves and slave owners. Being a Christian is about being like Jesus, and sometimes that means taking risks to reach out. He asks us to take on flesh and shake hands with the world. Sure, it's hard to respond to the pain around us. We'd so much rather be at the weddings than the funerals. But the call of compassion, of shared mourning, means we must get dirty. No hand-sanitizer Christianity. Sometimes it is unpleasant. Who wants to spend a day with a friend holding their head and wiping their face after a chemo treatment? Who wants to listen to the grief wails of a new widow or hear the drama of a husband whose wife just left him? Most of the time we'd all prefer to drive by and let someone else change the person's flat tire.

This idea of being willing to step into someone else's pain or even risk danger to relieve someone's agony reminds me of movie scenes where a military leader asks for volunteers for a dangerous mission or a ship's captain asks for people to stay on the sinking liner to help others get into the life rafts. It reminds me of a boss who foregoes his salary to give a paycheck to the employees he loves. Jesus pleads with us, calls us out, and invites us to get gritty.

It's exhausting and often unpleasant, but on the other hand, when I think of the times when I've most felt the cocooning of the Holy Spirit, it is when I've gone to another with comfort. Afterward I've felt a peace settle over me. Psychologists sometimes call this "the helper's high."

Sadly, I've missed the blessing of being a blessing more than a few times. I regret this. The other day, during a staff meeting prayer time, we began talking about how superficial most churches are—how most Christians don't really want to expose their junk and need for real help, and also how most pastors really don't want to go that deep. In the middle of the discussion, our worship leader and very close friend started to show some rare emotion as he said, "Hugh, remember the night my wife was really sick, and I tried to call you for help? Then I texted you and told you how bad she was, and then you finally texted me back saying, 'Bro, I'm sorry I didn't pick up the phone. I didn't know how bad it was.' Well, it really hurt me that you screened my call, knowing the kind of frightening time we were having with her health."

As he began to tremble in front of our staff, he continued, "That night was the worst of my life, and I knew you were busy, tired, and slammed with other pressures, but you were the person I most needed to pick up the phone. You are one of my best friends." I had no response other than to mourn my own lack of compassion.

Sometimes the call to dive into the pain of another requires a long commitment, but other times it simply requires you to be accessible and to pick up the phone, share a few words of comfort, and listen. Mourning is about being "present" with people while they hurt.

I missed God's ways that night my friend needed me, and it will be something I regret for the rest of my life. Thankfully, other times I get it right.

Jesus's call is for us to be tuned in to pain, weeping with those who weep and rejoicing with those who rejoice.

The Problem with Family Values

Since we've been in Denver now about seven years, I've had many people ask if we like it as much as we enjoyed Portland. My response is usually, "We miss the culture of Portland, but we love the Colorado weather."

Portland culture comes down to the unique style of people from the Northwest. You won't find as many national restaurant chains as you will in other places. There's a local coffee shop, bakery, or pub on just about every corner. Each neighborhood has a distinct flavor of unique people. And the place is full of eclectics, artists, witches, warlocks, skinheads, and other assorted nonevangelical types. As someone who enjoys people who color outside societal norms, for me, it was like getting a free pass to Disneyland. Okay, maybe Disneyland of the druids, but still—I cannot say I was ever bored by the people I encountered there.

Denver is different. People come here to play. Paganism runs deep, but it's veiled in recreational opportunities; the arts; city life; Broncos, Avs, and Rockies games; nice homes; golf courses; and travel. Although Denver now leads Portland in microbreweries (which gives me solace), it still feels pretty conservative.

When people ask me, "What's the hardest part of leading a church?" or "What is the most frustrating cultural hurdle to leap?" my answer comes easily. It's not competition with the Denver Broncos playing on TV or the sunny weather and perfectly groomed ski slopes on Sunday morning. It's not the fact that the most affluent suburbs are now as unchurched as left-wing Boulder County, or the fact that we lead the nation in per capita singleness or alcohol abuse. Nope, the one nagging, consistent hindrance to people finding and living out a vibrant kingdom life is . . . midwestern "family first" values.

Many people in Denver are transplants from Texas, Nebraska, Wyoming, Iowa, the Dakotas, and Missouri. Redneck, red meat, red state "aliens"! These people hail from places where a slow life, family values, and few words form the culture. These are great folks, but it has been hard to get them to do two important things Jesus people are supposed to do. One is to talk! Privacy is paramount in many midwestern cultures. The other is to give up some family time, especially on Sundays.

Maybe it's due to their ingrained politeness and reserved heritage. Maybe they feel it is inappropriate to expose inner thoughts, past mistakes, or longings for more adventure. In our town, just down the road from Focus on the Family, having abundant time alone with your family is considered the "godly" way to live. I have found it difficult to get these dear folks to engage the culture at large, be it leaving the pot roast and taters with Uncle Earl to go hang with some neighbors or new friends or initiating more than a two-sentence dialogue with others outside their most immediate (and usually blood-related) circle.

In the Northwest, we just figure everyone's family is already broken into a million dysfunctional pieces, so we have nothing better to do on the weekends than bring out some good microbrew, pour some Pinot Noir, gather 'round the fire, and let the conversation begin!

In short, the reason it was easier to dive into Northwest culture is that the people were more open. It's much harder to dive into the broken places of people who work hard to keep it together and whose default is one of privacy and protecting their image.

Although I am mostly joking about these cultural generalizations, Jesus seemed to have a similar problem getting people to reach out beyond their own close-knit family circles. In Jesus's day a typical Friday found most families gathering several generations together to prepare the Sabbath meal. Then they spent the entire day together on Saturday. It was like watching the scene in *My Big Fat Greek Wedding* where the uncle brings a whole lamb from the butcher shop and the wives all work tirelessly preparing a Dodge truck full of enough food to feed a small Greek army. Families in the time of Christ stayed each to their own. They would see other families walking to the service at the synagogue, but they'd quietly return home for a private meal. Very little contact was made with other Jewish families, and virtually no contact was made with Gentiles or pagans. To do the latter would have been to risk sin.

It's against this backdrop that Jesus takes his disciples over to visit the home of a tax collector named Levi. Levi was an outcast. His job as a tax collector isolated him from the locals, and every Sabbath eve you would have found him home alone. Although Jesus seemed to have a knack for getting into trouble on the Sabbath (by closing the rule book to offer aid to the hurting), sharing a home-cooked meal with this social leper would have been beyond mind-boggling. But Jesus went where he knew there was a need, without regard for societal norms.

There's another odd story in Scripture in which Jesus seems to mess with some major family-only, family-first rules. Jesus is talking to the multitudes, and his mother and brothers are standing outside asking to speak to him. Rather than stop his teaching, he incorporates the request and includes the crowd in his response, "Who is my mother, and who are my brothers?" Then he said, pointing to his disciples, "Here are my mother and my brothers. For whoever does the will of my Father in heaven is my brother and sister and mother" (Matt. 12:48–50).

So what's up with that? Is compassionate Christ suddenly missing a sensitivity gene? Where are his priorities?

Note that he did not say to his family, "I am disowning you and abandoning you for this audience." He was not excluding anyone. And that is the point, actually. He was telling his relatives that this crowd of people needed him right now, and spiritually speaking, they were his family. He loved them enough to include them in his family circle. It was a lesson in widening the family doors, opening the family hearth, giving up some private time to redefine the meaning of "family." In God's eyes we are all his children, all equally wanted and invited to the family table. "God places the solitary in families and gives the desolate a home in which to dwell," says the psalmist (Ps. 68:6 AMP).

Opening Up Our Families

Hospitality actually means "love of strangers," and believe me, Eastern hospitality trumps Southern hospitality—as sweet as it is—any day.

I see this scenario all the time. A couple gets married and they isolate themselves from important friends, sometimes Christians, but usually their non-Christian friends. When they have a child they either hide out or head to grandma's house every spare minute for help. If they have more kids, they move to the burbs and take a whole decade or two off from any real commitment to reach others outside their immediate family, using the old "we're focusing on our kids right now" card.

Look, I know times are tough. I'm a big family guy myself. I love my wife and kids and time at home with them. I get it. And I know you have to work hard to just stay afloat (trust me, I'm there too), and it takes a ton of time and energy to raise kids today in American culture. To help your kids succeed by worldly standards, you'll want to get them involved in everything, overcommit them, and overwork them, all so they can get ahead. I realize that at the end of the week, it's tough enough to load the minivan up with a bunch of whiny kids to be at church. I know it's just easier to sleep in and then head to the in-laws' for lunch. And here I am, encouraging you to open your home and engage in the lives of disoriented or hurting people. Where are you supposed to fit *that* in the family schedule? Okay, here's a few helpful hints, free of charge (well, other than what you plunked down for this book).

First, don't buy in to everything the world calls "success." Success isn't necessarily making it to college or attaining a nice home. Many have spent all their energy doing this and ended up with nothing more than additional stress. If you took the traditional ladder to the top and it only led you to a marginal spiritual fervor and commitment, then why do you want to pass that "legacy" along to your children? Is your greatest goal that they end up with a life exactly like yours? In truth, psychologists are seeing stressed-out children in droves because they are being asked to start up the ladder of success at, oh, about age five. Too many activities, lessons, classes, sports, even religious events make our kids into stressed-out mini-adults. Busyness is *not* next to godliness. And it's building in us and our children the habit of not engaging hurting people.

Jesus came to expand your life, not keep it the same. His life is fuller than the American dream, but it's not as safe. The way of Jesus includes commitment to your family, but it also calls you to fling open the doors of your home to strangers, the brokenhearted, and the lonely. So what I'm suggesting is this: cut out some of the nonstop activities and make room for a few more people in your family room. Keep margin in your life, blank days on your calendar, and flexibility in your spare time so that you can adopt a few "orphans" into your life.

Cheryl and I are no different from you. Although committed to full-time ministry, we've never made even close to a full paycheck from it. I've often had to work two to three jobs to make ends meet, and my son's constant epilepsy has kept us sleep-deprived and emotionally drained for the entire twenty-three years of his life. Yet we've seen God's faithfulness to us as we've stayed open for him to use our lives. Although tired, we've regularly opened our home for friends and drop-ins. Although broke, we're happy to buy extra food and wine and then set another plate (or six) at the table. Although some of our extended family sends us occasional emails and phone calls rebuking us for not participating in every single family function, we recognize our limitations. We show up at some events, sure, but we leave room for our home to be a place of hospitality for friends as well as seekers in search of a place to belong.

Every Thanksgiving our table is surrounded by disconnected stragglers alongside the Halter five. We love it and believe it pleases the Lord. In truth, our kids wouldn't have it any other way. Their lives are richer from the flow of folks who come in and out of our home. Because our kids were raised in an open home, they think of this as a normal way to do family life.

From Small Groups to Incarnational Communities

Another area that will be affected by the call to mourn will be our classic church small groups. I know this is ultrasacrilegious, but I don't like small groups! Never have, probably never will, and I'm not so sure Jesus would give up a good episode of *24* to join one either. Let me explain.

As we now realize, Jesus was bent on "opening up the family." You might assume, therefore, that I'd be jumping up and down to applaud the concept of subfamilies we typically call "small groups." A lot of churches have them, and they're designed to give Christian people a chance to do more of what they did on Sunday, only smaller. A place to learn more Scripture and be with believers, only you get a chance to talk more. What could be wrong with that?

When a young couple comes to our church looking to be "plugged in" to one of our missional communities or "villages" (which they assume are set up like small groups in the churches they have been to before), I ask them to consider the hundreds of people in their neighborhoods who may need a true friend. Then I pose this question: "What do you think about letting God help you become a place of belonging for others instead of you just looking for another place to belong?" Some people love this and admit that they've always wanted to take this challenge seriously; they truly wish they could begin to reach out to those already in their circle of relationships or neighborhood.

But not everyone understands the difference. Missional communities have, well, a "mission": to create belonging for others beyond themselves. Small groups don't. In order to create belonging, these incarnational communities force people to deal with their own issues of individualism, consumerism, and materialism as they interact with others potentially unlike themselves. Small groups don't. Most importantly, incarnational communities have a mission together for those outside the faith. Small groups usually don't.

Old school small groups place an empty chair in the middle of the room and pray that God would fill it. But a kingdom-minded community of friends, intent on living like Jesus, will choose together to seek those who mourn and place chairs for themselves among the lonely, hurting, and broken.

Learning from the Johnsons

Part of any good writing experience is working with an editor. Becky Johnson is a friend who helped me with this book. As I was about to send her this chapter for review, before I pressed "Send" I began to think about how she and her husband, Greg, have exemplified this call to mourn. Becky is as Texas as it comes. Deeply committed to her family, Becky has a hot meal simmering on the stove every day and wouldn't miss a chance to fly to her family or fly her family in to be together. And a lot of her kids and grandkids live near enough to drop in and pull up a chair for a glass of iced tea and conversation. But Becky and Greg have also modeled a prolific sense of opening their family to the larger family God is building. Each week they dive into the deep struggles of young couples and hurting individuals. Not a month goes by when we don't laugh and commiserate in sadness over the pain of all the "adopted family" to whom they are opening their wallets, their schedules, and their home.

As their pastor, I often have to ask them to make sure they are taking time for themselves and not letting the needs of others overwhelm them, but they just keep mourning with those who mourn—or as Becky likes to put it, "companioning those in a season of sorrow" until they are more whole again.

Once this life is over, we will never again have to be sad, cry, or carry someone's burdens. Life will be like a big family feast or the perfect small group. This life, however, is full of both joy and pain. As we experience the comfort of others in our own times of pain, our call is to pass the empathy and love forward. For the serious apprentice of Jesus, over the years of our own struggles, we become more sensitive to those who are wincing and bent over in pain—and we carry their burden with them until it lightens to a manageable load.

This is the living sermon that the world longs to see.

 To consider: Try to remember a time in your life when someone chose to mourn with you. How important was it to you?

 To consider: When planning your free time and weekends, do you have any consistent pattern of opening your home?

 To do: Commit one hour a week of service to someone who is struggling.

 To do: Make a commitment to someone who is stuck in a pattern of mournful life. Take action such as tutoring an inner-city youth or working in a ministry for battered women or homeless people.

"These past days the tragedies of broken lives have been full. I should like ultimately to have a home where those in 'the blues' could come, not so much to be talked to as to be, or to wander around until healing comes to them."

Oswald Chambers

6

THE ART OF SUBTLE WOOING

Winning the World through Meekness

Blessed are the meek,
for they will inherit the earth.
Matthew 5:5

Two years ago I received the best gift ever: a Harley David-
son Dyna Super Glide. It had been a twenty-year dream to
have a bike of this quality, so I was in Easy Rider heaven
when I hit the open road, wind whistling over my bald head.

Of all the benefits of Harley ownership, I was initially most
impressed by the new "community" into which I had been
adopted. When you belong to this community, you get to participate in the secret and just barely observable Harley wave.
This wave occurs when you are passing another Harley rider
on the road. Unlike, for example, the beauty pageant wave,

95

or the wave you give someone as you greet them when they come into view at the airport, a Harley wave is not flamboyant. Most men don't like to wave at other men anyway, but some sign of cool camaraderie seemed necessary, so a simple hand slowly lowered in a downward direction evolved as the secret signal. When you see another rider initiate this wave from across the intersection or across the freeway divider, it's almost rude not to reciprocate.

The first couple months, I actually went out looking for my "brothers." The rougher the guys looked, the cooler I felt interacting with them.

One day, however, I was presented with an interesting dilemma. I was stopped at a red light. Directly across the intersection was another rider. There were no other cars, just me and this rogue cyclist. He was atop a Suzuki scooter and sporting a 1970s, orange, open-face helmet with a sleeveless denim vest. I tried to act as though I didn't see him, but every time I looked forward, he waved at me. Not the cool Harley wave but an overhand, sideways, high school cheerleader wave.

I was stunned.

Emotionally paralyzed.

I didn't know what to do.

The awkwardness persisted, as no other cars showed up to relieve the pressure. I tried to look to the side, but I could see Suzuki boy in my periphery, still focused on me expectantly. I breathed a few sighs, and then I just looked at the guy. He, of course, waved again, but I just sat there, unresponsive, trying to let my nonverbals communicate, "Yo, dude, you're not my people." He eventually got the drift, and we both waited awkwardly for the light to change. I'm not proud of the moment, mind you, but I just couldn't—by a girly wave of my hand—agree that we were in the same cool motorcycle brotherhood. Just could not do it.

Maybe you know the feeling. Have you ever wanted to disassociate from a group of people that represented you? Maybe a family member, a co-worker, a teammate, or maybe even other Christians? Clearly, we have all at times brought reproach and embarrassment to our parents, our spouse, our kids, or a coach we represent, and so we can't take potshots at people who have a bad day occasionally. But I think it's okay to acknowledge that there is a tribe within the Christian family that it's just really hard to identify with. They're the ones who offend your friends, wear Christian T-shirts, and think Rush Limbaugh is the clean-up hitter, just after Jesus, Mother Teresa, and Billy Graham. They're the folks who wouldn't miss a Sunday church service, but you hope they never meet your churchless friends. They use weird words like *midst*, *glory*, *bountiful*, and *presence* and say "Amen" at really inappropriate times.

In eighth grade I was at a pizza party when a teammate was flipping through the TV channels and came upon a Christian station with flamboyant preachers and cheesy music. I saw it out of the corner of my eye but acted like I was just eating pizza, hoping he wouldn't pause on that channel. Sure enough, he not only stopped the channel surfing but said, "Hey Hugh, aren't you a Christian like these wackos?" That was just one of the hundreds of times I've had to grovel, defend, or just flat-out apologize for certain parts of the Christian family.

Now, the Christian family is quite large, and we've got about as many different personalities and characters as the Waltons or, probably more appropriately, the Simpsons. Two of our relatives, in particular, need some explaining.

The first is the evangelicals. My guess is that many who hear that word immediately have a negative reaction because it sounds like *evangelism*, a word that conjures up nauseating experiences like "trying to save someone," "convert them," "preach at them," or "going door to door." If you've ever been on the receiving end of one of these things, then the word *evangelical* may give you the hives or a sudden desire to become invisible. If you've been on the giving end, your reaction may not be much better.

A Brief History of Two Recent Christian Movements

We'll get back to the "saving people" thing in a bit, but I think you should know where evangelicalism began and how this tribe of Christians came to be.

To evangelize actually means to "good news" someone. Early Christians felt honored and thrilled to explain the message of this new world that was opening up to them because of Jesus. Within this message was embedded the possibility of racial and ethnic reconciliation, physical and emotional healing, hope against injustice, power against tyranny and dark spiritual forces, hope for an afterlife, and pure acceptance by God. In this happy context, *evangelism* was a good word, as it should still be today.

Interestingly, evangelicalism didn't appear until the mid-eighteenth century in England. Arriving on the heels of the Protestant Reformation, the evangelical movement urged Christians to take the call to "good news" people seriously. Because the church (both Catholic and Protestant) was pulpit-focused and because a large portion of the population was in a church on Sunday, evangelicals put a lot of emphasis on good-news-ing people through preaching. They focused on simple teaching through the Bible, covering themes such as sin, conversion, heart transformation, and personal salvation.

The early evangelicals and those who brought the same fervor to the New World believed in good-news-ing people by offering others practical help. For example, the abolition movement began under George Whitefield in England and later continued under William Wilberforce. Whitefield came to the colonies and helped start what was known as the First Great Awakening. Out of this awakening, the good-news-ing continued, thousands upon thousands did convert or have a change of heart, and the evangelical Christian movement not only captured the country with personal faith but brought forth a tidal wave of social reform that strengthened America. Prison reform, hospitals, and institutions of higher learning were just a few of the reasons evangelical Christians were held in high esteem. The secular world at large was thankful for their work to make each city safe, healthy, and productive. They were thankful for evangelicals.

So why do modern-day evangelicals get such a bad rap? To understand that you have to deal with another word: fundamentalists. For many Christians, these are the dudes at life's intersection that you often don't want to wave at. Let me explain.

In the early 1900s secularism was on the move, especially in our colleges and universities. The trustworthiness of the Scriptures was under attack. People who were antichurch believed that if you could disprove the viability of the Holy Scriptures, you could do away with Christianity.

Out of this fight emerged a group of evangelicals who initially succeeded in dispelling the secular-atheist attempt to challenge fundamental doctrines like the need for an atoning Savior, the virgin birth, and the resurrection. Those who stood for these fundamental truths were naturally called "fundamentalists." Initially most of us probably would have loved these people too. But as the years went on, the fundamentalist movement grew more defensive, retreated from public life, and viewed themselves as the remnant who were the only true Christians. A people who used to woo and win the world's ear were now quickly becoming the people you least wanted to share a meal, a pint, or the back seat of your Harley with. In time, fundamentalists began to make a large percentage of their Christian cousins squirm uneasily.

Fundamentalist preaching was no longer about "good news"; it was more inflammatory and insecure, culminating in what we would call "fire and brimstone" preaching. The Good News of Christ's payment for our sin, his immeasurable grace for every sinner, and his call for Christians to become revolutionaries who bring kingdom life to the streets was less emphasized, as the focus in preaching shifted to fear-based dramatic sermons about the horrors of hell.

Judgment replaced love. Churches became viewed as God's tools to stand up for truth—to the point that they were willing to beat people down instead of being his instrument of blessing, love, and forgiveness. As the vocal and increasingly well-funded mouthpieces for God, some leaders focused on calling out "wrong" behavior, accepting only perfect holiness, and felt no need to be sensitive with a world clearly going to hell in a handbasket. Their approach was, "Just give 'em the truth. If they don't turn, let 'em burn." The more the emphasis was on judgment rather than grace, the more calloused Christians became to their fellow man.

Fundamentalism became the enemy of the culture and, not surprisingly, adopted a political agenda that emphasized outward behavior rather than an inward need for change. Many prominent pastors took public positions on "moral" issues, creating pressure for folks in the pews to "fight against" society. Through highly charged rhetoric that aroused emotional responses, these leaders raised millions of dollars for their "cause," making it very clear they were choosing to engage in a culture war rather than win hearts by incarnating the ways of the kingdom.

I took a detour to share this oversimplified history of evangelicalism and fundamentalism to say this: you don't have to be a fundie to follow Jesus, and you don't have to acknowledge them as like-minded compatriots from across the intersection. In fact, you really don't have to identify yourself as either a fundamentalist or an evangelical. I am merely pointing out some history so that you understand how the world has viewed different strains of Christians. I also don't want you to think anything is inherently wrong with being evangelical or taking fundamental stances on certain issues. But I do hope you now see the danger that exists when we fail to see our beliefs in the context of the culture we're in. Remember, people followed Jesus for roughly 1900 years without any evangelical or fundamentalist designations, and I would encourage you to start fresh without all the baggage.

I "fundamentally" base my life on the Holy Scriptures and have strong convictions about what Jesus is showing me, but I now realize I don't have to be an oppressive, insecure, offensive fundie to be a Christian. There's a way to follow God in the way of Jesus and win the world with the original message of Good News.

I hope to show that this is why Jesus calls us to meekness in this Beatitude: "Blessed are the meek, for they will inherit the earth" (Matt. 5:5).

Before I give a few words on what it means to be meek, let me explain what I think it means to "inherit the earth."

Inherit the Earth

As with all of Jesus's new concepts about kingdom people, there seems to be an order to heavenly principles that is the exact opposite of earthly logic. The poor in spirit really do get heaven; those who mourn on earth really will receive God's comfort. And now Jesus tells the crowd that the meek will inherit the earth.

If you're like me, you may have wondered, "What's the big deal with *that* promise?"

It's huge.

And it all comes from a story any Jewish person would have identified with regarding the most important part of their national/religious heritage. Way back in Exodus, God's people were to "inherit" the Promised Land. It was a physical place that was beautiful and had everything the nation would need. But it also held deep metaphorical meaning for life with God.

In the middle drawer of my desk is a small ziplock bag that has a handful of white gravel in it. If you looked at it, you might ask, "Why in the world do you have that?" Well, it's a clump of dirt I scooped up just inside a thirty-foot wall that separates Palestinian Bethlehem from Israel a few miles

This picture was taken outside of Bethlehem. It is a beautifully painted depiction of Jerusalem on a thirty-foot wall that separates families, neighborhoods, countries, and the world. You see in the artist's rendition the land of Jerusalem. But what interests your eye first is the hands of Jesus making a way into the land. This picture powerfully speaks to the only answer for the complicated crisis in this land: that is, the gentle but powerful presence of Jesus, meek and mild. © Brad Corrigan

outside Jerusalem. This clump of dirt is in part why we experienced the horrors of 9/11. It has caused continual global unrest throughout the Middle East, Asia, Africa, and most strategic points of the world. The fight for a mere one hundred miles of land has caused fear of terrorism, holy wars, and divided political factions in the United States over our support or nonsupport of certain countries.

Apparently land matters. The dirt in my desk holds significance. We in the West like land, but most of us would never allow generation after generation of our own children to face violence over a few thousand acres. If someone said, "I'm going to kill your family if you stay here, and by the way, we'll compensate you so you can relocate," almost all of us would start packing the minivan. But to others, who believe

This photo captures Scripture painted on the same wall.
© Brad Corrigan

that their claim on certain areas of land (both Jewish and Palestinian) was given to them by God directly, leaving would feel like walking away from God at best and contributing to the end of your people at worst. In the Middle Eastern mind-set, giving up their territory is simply not a viable option.

Jesus the humble and meek, who climbed down out of heaven to come and build a home in our neighborhood, is the answer for both the conflict in the Middle East and the wars fighting within every human heart. Jesus wants his people, his apprentices, to win—to see people changed and converted to his ways—but the methods of winning are just as important as the win itself, because they can't be separated. We win with meekness.

Winning the World through Meekness

Meekness is strength under control, power under restraint. It's the ability to be self-effacing. It is not shyness or insecurity; it's the opposite, actually. Meekness is a black belt in martial arts disarming a drunk through words instead of violence. Meekness is a trait the world has observed in people like Nelson Mandela, Martin Luther King Jr., Mahatma Gandhi, and Billy Graham, people who have incredible power but who have learned to harness that power through humility, servant-hood, and kindness instead of arrogance, power, or control.

One of the best pictures of Jesus's meekness is found in the story of a Roman centurion who was thrust into the last three days of Jesus's life. Like other centurions before him, this man was accustomed to hearing new Jewish would-be messiahs call out Roman powers. But this man, Jesus, didn't seem to be calling for a vote or running for election. He simply and comfortably talked about issues of the heart and about a new kingdom of God and of heaven.

As the crowds following Jesus continued to grow, Caiaphas, the high priest, became uneasy and asked the centurion to lead the arrest of Jesus in Gethsemane. In a knee-jerk reaction to Christ's arrest, Peter did what any good Jew would expect and lopped off the ear of the high priest's servant (see John 18:10). The soldier surely expected a Roman-Jewish throwdown, but it didn't happen. Jesus not only kept the riot from breaking out but actually put the guy's ear back on, essentially saying something like, "Hey, sorry, man, our bad . . . here you go, it's all fixed."

This rugged soldier likely felt strangely curious about Jesus's inner strength and exterior gentleness. After he took Jesus to the powers in charge, he watched as hour by hour they brutalized Jesus in every conceivable humiliating way. He saw Jesus take the abuse without whimpering or pleading for relief. Each fist that pounded his face, each time spit splattered against his mouth and eyes, each insult was met with a determined but quiet gaze. Then came the execution.

Spikes tore through his flesh; a crown of daggers dug into his skull; jeers of past worshipers mocked him. And then words that he could never have imagined would come from a man . . . any man: "Father, forgive them, for they do not know what they are doing" (Luke 23:34). A few moments later he heard Jesus say, "It is finished" (John 19:30).

At this moment perhaps the skeptical Roman warrior bent down, took off his helmet, and dropped his sword as

The Art of Subtle Wooing

he proclaimed, "Surely this man was the Son of God" (Mark 15:39). This, my friends, is the epitome of the power of meekness to reach the world. Jesus in his power could have come down off the cross and proven his might, then forced allegiance from his torturers and belittled the ignorant. But instead we see Jesus, our example, teaching us how to "win" the world. And as Jesus now tries to teach us what being his apprentice will mean, we're going to have to try our hand at life his way. For he said, "Take my yoke upon you, and learn of me; for I am meek and lowly in heart" (Matt. 11:29 KJV).

The Power of Posture

When I was in college, I took a class on "the psychology of communication." One point stood out to me, and I've found it to be true in all situations: nonverbal communication is the most powerful form of communication. What is seen communicates more than what is actually said. For instance, if I have been really busy, working so much that I barely have any time for Cheryl or the kids, and then notice that Cheryl seems upset, I can ask, "Honey, is everything okay?" If she says, "Everything is fine," but I notice she is looking down at the ground or says it as she walks outside and shuts the door in my face, I have learned that it's actually *not fine!* Her nonverbal communication is coming through loud and clear.

Words tell people what we think, but our actions, our facial expressions, our touch, or our general "posture" tells people what we actually feel. And this is the power of Jesus to win the hearts of people. When the woman was caught in adultery, Jesus postured himself as an advocate for her, kneeling down beside her as she was stooped over under the condemnation of the pious. When Jesus quietly allowed Mary to pour valuable perfumed oil over his head while skeptics belittled her, he was communicating his compassion for this woman. When he turned tables over by the temple, the sound of crashing trinkets and the look on his face communicated far more powerfully than the words people heard him mutter. As he reclined at Levi's table, laughing and enjoying dinner with the outcasts, people picked up on his inclusive love. Most starkly, the fact that Jesus lived in the neighborhood for thirty years without letting people know he was their Savior, their Messiah, their God, and instead just lived with them, celebrated with them, and mourned with them, is astounding. His voice and words would someday, in the right timing, cut their hearts to the core, but his ability to draw a crowd and win the crowd was based on his beautiful posture, his nonverbals. And we would do well to live the same way.

In the book of Philippians, Paul encourages us to be like Jesus, who—though being all-powerful—intentionally chose not to force the issue with us or force dogma down our throats. Instead he chose to live among us, love us, show us and teach us about how to live life in his new kingdom. It's incredible that in the three years of his ministry recorded in Scripture, we don't see him aggressively trying to convert anyone. He just seemed to wait for them to come to him. This is the power of godly posture.

To me, this is all the proof I need that God doesn't want us to stick up for him, confound the unchurched with our right doctrine, or belittle them with attempts to be morally superior. Jesus is teaching us to stop trying to convert people and begin wooing them to his kingdom way of life through the meekness of our way. Meekness will cause us to be dignified and in turn dignify the spiritual journeys of others. Meekness will compel us to respect others, listen to them, and acknowledge the things that turn them off about Christians, especially if they've had a few run-ins with fundies. Meekness by its very definition communicates to people an authentic belief that we aren't any better than they are—really!—and that we only know what we know and have changed because God pursued us, saved us, helped us, and loved us.

Yes, Jesus did teach about the need to be born again spiritually. He did confront people with their need to repent of sin. And so will we . . . if we win their hearts through the power of meekness. With meekness, evangelism and our heartfelt desire to see our friends find Jesus become like one homeless person helping another homeless person find a warm bed for the night.

Exchanging Aggression for Meekness

So here's a real switcheroo. Evangelicals need to learn that the earliest and most prolific communities of Jesus followers, who saw literally thousands of their friends come to faith in one day and who turned entire cities around for Jesus, were not, as a general rule, aggressive toward the culture. Instead they simply waited for people to come with their curiosity and questions. In 1 Peter 3:15–16, Peter said, "Always be prepared to give an answer to everyone who asks you to give the reason for the hope that you have. But do this with gentleness and respect, keeping a clear conscience, so that those who speak maliciously against your good behavior in Christ may be ashamed of their slander."

We should ask ourselves, "Is anyone asking me about my life or my faith?" If not, I think Jesus would say, "Then you're not living out the level of love I called you to in this life." Often we think people's lack of spiritual response is because they just don't want to find God. More often, I have found, the real problem is that we just don't live enough like Jesus yet.

Think about this. In early New Testament times, the most religious people, the Pharisees, were highly evangelistic, sometimes sailing across far seas to win one convert. But here is what Jesus said to them in Matthew 23:15: "Woe to you, teachers of the law and Pharisees, you hypocrites! You travel over land and sea to win a single convert, and when you have succeeded, you make them twice as much a child of hell as you are."

Conversion isn't just about helping someone find faith. Yes, it includes this, but when people focus all their efforts on getting people "saved," they communicate only a small part of the Good News. All too often we are like egomaniacs wanting to turn converts into evangelists, like a giant pyramid scheme where the main goal of the corporation is to multiply and get more warm bodies in the door. But Jesus does not need any more arrogant soul-winners who go out to make more arrogant soul-winners. Jesus wants us to point people to who he really was—a man of humility and love—then allow that image to change them in whatever way God wants. It is not a cookie-cutter operation. The Good News is that every person has a story, and the way Jesus enters each story is highly unique and individual. The process may take years to complete, with fits of starts and stops and doubts along the way. God never meant for us to sign people up with a quick prayer, a contract, and a pat on the back. He intended for us to love and journey with others in their walk toward and with Jesus. This isn't about a duty to be performed; it is about a relationship to be explored.

Jesus's own apprentices at first didn't get his lesson about approaching others with humility. In Luke 9, the disciples were in a fight over who was the greatest dude among them, which Jesus basically dismissed by saying, "It is the one who is least among you all who is the greatest" (v. 48), which probably didn't sound like a lot of fun to them. Then Jesus sent word to the Samaritans that he was coming through town, but the Samaritans didn't respond favorably. So what did these self-focused, power-hungry apprentices do? They asked Jesus, like the tough guys they wanted to be, a question I can only hear in my head as sounding like one of the Sopranos: "Yo, Jesus! You wanna we should call down fire on dose blasted pagan half-breeds?"

And they asked this right after Christ's little lesson on humility.

You have to wonder if Jesus hit his forehead and thought, "Oy veh!" There's no biblical record of that, but Luke does record that Jesus rebuked them for their attitude of assumed superiority (see 9:51–56).

Living Witnesses

On one of my plane trips a few years ago, a young twenty-something guy sat next to me. We were just getting settled, and I made the mistake of mentioning the smell of the Subway sandwich that he had just tucked into his seat-back pocket. I said, "The smell of the fresh bread is making me hungry," to which he replied, "You know, bread is a powerful metaphor for the life of Jesus. Did you know that Jesus called himself the bread of life?" He kept going, but as I realized that he was trying to "convert" me, I thought I'd play along and act the role of any good pagan.

I cleared my throat and earnestly asked, "So what part of Jesus do you think the cold cuts and soggy lettuce represent?" Stammering for some theological response, he made some mention of how they probably didn't have lettuce back then but might have substituted olives, which of course represented something Jesus-y. For the next hour, I kept working him over pretty good, but finally I couldn't take it anymore and told him I was a pastor.

He looked mortified. "So you were just pretending?"

"Yep."

"So how'd I do?"

"Well, quite frankly, you lost me at hello with the 'bread of life' hook. It not only was pretty lame but actually got lamer as you went on. Not only would you not have converted me, but if I weren't a pastor, I probably would have requested a seat change, preferably with someone in the mental health profession who could be of more help to you." He laughed, then relaxed a bit. From there we actually had a good talk about what an effective "witness" really looks like.

When Jesus called his followers to be witnesses, he was asking them to allow their lives to tell the story of his life. He wanted their actions, their community, their values, their love and kindness, and their visible transformation to be the most powerful way to communicate God's heart to the world.

In 2 Corinthians 3:2–3 Paul says, "You yourselves are our letter, written on our hearts, known and read by everyone. You show that you are a letter from Christ, the result of our ministry, written not with ink but with the Spirit of the living God, not on tablets of stone but on tablets of human hearts." Witnessing is about being read, not reading yourself aloud (on a soapbox) to others. It's much more about visible witness than about verbal witness, especially these days when people are generally jaded, often for good reason. Postmodern people believe what they see, not what they hear. There's always plenty of time for talking heart-to-heart about the central Good News, but first we need to let "the letter of a life well lived" be so radically loving that others will invite us to share our thoughts, rather than us forcing our opinions on them.

To the small church in Thessalonica, Paul reported that their love in action "rang out" (1 Thess. 1:8) throughout the entire countryside like an echo—something that reverberated everywhere. You don't have to keep beating the world over the head with the Good News. When we live the gospel well so that people can "read it in our lives," it is like a musical note played so clearly that it keeps reverberating and spreading from person to person in the most natural way. Like kindness, it keeps being paid forward.

What exactly was the message that was being echoed from the Thessalonians? It was positive gossip about their transformation, their faith, how they turned away from idolatry to serve God. Some may assume it was their doctrine—that their message of Christ's godhood, life, death, resurrection, and return was what bounced all over the world. But it wasn't. Paul specifically tells us it was their communal reputation, how they lived, that caused such a buzz on the grapevine. The message of the gospel made sense as it lined up with the life of the gospel.

There's a great scene in Acts 16 where a woman is walking behind Paul, proclaiming Paul's message to people. I think of her as the really overzealous Christians who come up after you preach a message so they can preach another message to you. She was proclaiming the Word. You would assume Paul would be thrilled that he had some fellow "proclaimers" at his side. But, well, read for yourself the story and what he does:

> Once when we were going to the place of prayer, we were met by a female slave who had a spirit by which she predicted the future. She earned a great deal of money for her owners by fortune-telling. She followed Paul and the rest of us, shouting, "These men are servants of the Most High God, who are telling you the way to be saved." She kept this up for many days. Finally Paul became so annoyed that he turned around and said to the spirit, "In the name of Jesus Christ I command you to come out of her!" At that moment the spirit left her. (vv. 16–18)

I think it's funny Paul put up with this irritating "proclaimer" for several days. My guess is that he, like many of us, wondered whether he should challenge her or just let it go. Well, he eventually cracked. He turned around and essentially said, "Geez, lady, get the freak out of my space! You're killing me!" More accurately, he recognized that the spirit within her is not from God but is either a demon or from her own pressing need for attention. Just because someone is thumping the same Bible we read, using "Christian phrases" to impress themselves and others, doesn't necessarily mean they are honoring Christ.

If someone you meet doesn't respect you, don't talk about your faith. Just love and show. And don't be surprised if you have to love a lot more than you thought you would before they give you the time of day. The wall between Christ followers and those fed up with religious hypocrisy is thick and high. They're weary of our rhetoric, judgment, exclusiveness, and hypocrisy. The walls won't come tumbling down with a few good deeds. The wall of assumptions will only come down as entire communities band together in unity to live like Christ before the world. This may mean turning from idols of materialism, individualism, consumerism, and religion.

I'm sure I'll get emails from people challenging me about the need to say more about the gospel and to say it more often, but I believe the evidence is overwhelming that the problem of the church's decline and decay is not because our doctrine is hidden or inaccessible. We've got a street cred problem, a posture problem. We've been preaching our brains out for a hundred-plus years in churches on every corner. We have 24-7 television, radio, and internet preaching, teaching, and training that is in plain view of anyone who is willing to just watch or listen. But they don't.

I recommend an experiment. Most churches in America see one or two adults a year, at best, come to faith in Christ, so we're not risking much to change things up a bit. Consider as a community the challenge of not saying anything about Jesus to your sojourning friends unless asked. No Bible verses or doctrine for an entire year. Instead, replace that religious fervency with service, blessing, and an invitation to join a community where anyone can be real and relaxed and loved and cared about. At the end of the year, measure the results. You will not only find that your "street cred" increases but also be blown away at how often you get to talk about your faith.

Jesus Saves ... We Don't

So, you may be wondering, how do people come to faith? To start, mull over these five times Jesus grants salvation to people:

1. To the woman called "sinner" who anoints Jesus's feet with her tears and oil, Jesus said, "Your faith has saved you; go in peace" (Luke 7:50).
2. To the woman caught in adultery, he said, "Neither do I condemn you. . . . Go now and leave your life of sin" (John 8:11).
3. In Luke 5:20, as friends of a paralytic lower their sick friend through an opening in a roof, Jesus said, "Your sins are forgiven."

4. Luke 19 records Zacchaeus the tax collector offering to pay back money he'd taken from the peasants, and Jesus said, "Today salvation has come to this house" (v. 9).
5. In Luke 23 the thief being crucified next to Jesus said, "Jesus, remember me when you come into your kingdom." Jesus replied, "Truly I tell you, today you will be with me in paradise" (vv. 42–43).

In all of these examples, you'll notice no prayer, no altar call, no complete understanding about Jesus, no church to attend, no gospel tract with diagrams, and very little if any doctrinal understanding about Christ's payment for sin—and yet Jesus forgives these people's sins and invites them to be a part of his kingdom. What we see are honest transactions between people who were *drawn* to Jesus by his tangible heavenly ways. In my experience people tend to move toward God on their own. If they are given the chance to move *at their own pace*, they'll eventually gravitate toward a loving community and eventually come to love God too. Their doctrinal understanding will grow along with their relational connection to God's people.

I'm often asked what we should do if someone is interested in spiritual things but seems to believe in God outside our own Christian way of seeing God. "How should we confront them?" they ask. I usually respond, "Don't confront them. Instead, encourage their search. At least there is wind in their spiritual sails. Naturally they're sailing a little off course (like all of us), but fervency in a slightly immature direction is better than apathy in the right direction."

I've met Muslims who came to faith in Jesus by reading the Qur'an. I've known Hindus who found the Savior through botched self-mutilation attempts. I know quite a few New Agers who came to Christ when I encouraged them to keep seeking. Our Scriptures seem to indicate that even if we mess it up, the rocks will cry out and donkeys may start talking in

English! Jesus is the one who converts people and reorients the disoriented.

Jesus interacted with those who were unclear about their spiritual leanings, so you can be sure we all need to learn to help people process questions, opinions, and assumptions with grace, truth, tact, and patience. The deeper you and your communities engage the culture, the more colorful the conversations will be. The more authentic you become, the more honest they will be. The problems and issues people grapple with cannot be kept nice, neat, and tidy. The world is confusing, and issues of faith are no different.

The other day, during another hot yoga class I was taking, I was enjoying what students call the "child's pose." Essentially you lay on your face with your arms outstretched, palms up. After a long, hard workout, it's a welcome resting pose. As pleasant elevator music played, the instructor said, "Today as you quiet your heart and open your hands, receive wisdom. Breathe out anxiety and know that your life is being guided by someone who actually cares."

As I sat there, my face in a pool of sweat, I was blown away by the peace that came over me as I pondered *Jesus* because of this New Age instructor. After the class, I walked by the desk where she was sitting and said, "Wow . . . you really helped the pastor focus back on God today. Thank you very much."

"You're a pastor?" she asked, followed quickly by, "And I helped you focus on God?"

"Yep, you did. I have staked my whole future on the life of Jesus, but I fail in faith all the time and get all stressed out. This one hour with you every couple days is a place that really helps me center back on what I know." She smiled and so did I, and our conversations are getting deeper and more focused on Jesus all the time.

I have learned so much about God from doubters and others who are not Christians, sometimes in surprising and shocking ways. Listen deeply to others with whom you are sojourning in faith. Just because you may have been walking with Jesus for twenty or thirty years does not mean that your friend without faith or friend of a different faith will not also have spiritual truths to teach you. By taking a sincere posture of back-and-forth sharing of what you are both learning about God in your daily lives, you'll be earning a relational right to be heard.

Meekness will be the inner quality of a true apprentice, and it is a quality without which we can't help people to see and find God.

 To consider: Do people ever ask you about your life or beliefs? If not, do you think it is because you are not inspiring, approachable, or accessible?

 To do: Apologize to one person who you may have been too spiritually aggressive with.

"My Scandinavian roommate impressed me by his remarks in broken English when he came into my cabin last night. 'Ah, I see, your jokes and light-heartedness plough the land, then you put in the seeds. I feel in my insides, that this is right.'"

Oswald Chambers

7

GOD ON THE GO

Spiritual Formation between the Rubber and the Road

Blessed are those who hunger and thirst for righteousness,
for they will be filled.

Matthew 5:6

It was our first summer in Denver, and after taking a few months to get to know my neighbor Jeff, I finally decided to go over to his house to drum up a little male camaraderie. What I knew about Jeff was that he was really into cycling. He and his buddies would gather every Saturday morning for a long ride and then hang out afterward having a few beers. I'd go for the beers, but I felt like the only way to really get "in" with the crowd would be to take up the sport.

Jeff helped me buy my first road bike, and the next thing I knew I was at the top of a mountain puking my brains out.

Back home I lay horizontal on my front yard for four hours without moving. While staring up at the clouds, I vowed not to go with the team again until I was in a little better shape. Several weeks later, I felt ready to try a little longer ride. Jeff gave me a route and said it would take me "only" two hours or so.

I headed out. Then somewhere between purgatory and Sheol, I got lost in the foothills of the Rocky Mountains. Two hours in, after I polished off my last drink of water, I realized with profound clarity that I was in a bit of a pickle. The sun was beating down on me, and I had no more Clif Bars or fluids. Concerned, I headed for the small mountain town of Morrison where I crouched under a tree, trying not to pass out.

After coming to what was left of my senses, I stumbled over to a gas station and lapped up about five gallons of water from the scrungy bathroom sink (amazing how unpicky one gets about hygiene when one is dying of thirst). Still, I was completely void of energy with miles to go before I'd make it home. In fact, I would learn that I was experiencing what endurance athletes call "bonking," the term for when your body has depleted all its energy resources and is shutting down, like a laptop out of battery juice.

I rummaged through all my bags, hoping that maybe I'd missed a PowerBar, or even a stray peanut, just to get a little energy. But nary a piece of protein could I find. Nor did I have any spare change, a credit card, or any loose bills. I was jacked! Now any athlete who has bonked will tell you that in this condition, you can lose your ability to think clearly, so that's the excuse I'll give for what Pastor Halter did next.

I went back into the gas station, and while the distracted attendant took care of another patron, I lifted a bag of kettle chips and two Snickers bars, went back into the bathroom, sat on the toilet (I did have the presence of mind to put the seat down), and consumed the nutrients like a brand-new Shop-Vac. Ten seconds . . . done! Immediately I felt better.

My blood started to pump faster, my breathing came back to normal, my muscles started to strengthen, and then my mind started working just well enough for me to think, "What the . . . I just ripped off a convenience store!"

Of course I went back the next day and paid my tab. But I learned, like never before or since, the all-gripping power of true hunger and thirst.

I'm not sure if you've ever bonked physically, but if you're like most, you've probably bonked spiritually. In fact, this chapter will only make sense to those who have had seasons of long, drawn-out spiritual bankruptcy. Times when you just can't open the Scriptures. Weeks and months when you just can't muster the energy or faith to pray, even though you know you should, and when the absolute last place you want to be is at a church service on Sunday morning. During these times of desert spirituality we can become jaded about the meaning of Christian moralism, angry at the simplistic pat answers and nice neat bows tied on the end of every sermon, and distrusting of anything that promises easy spiritual growth.

So imagine how you might feel if you heard Jesus say, "Blessed are those who hunger and thirst for righteousness, for they will be filled" (Matt. 5:6).

Those sitting on the grass that day listening to Jesus were, as you can imagine, folks who had been controlled and constipated by religion, religious activity, and judgment at every turn. In truth, *righteousness* was a word they heard just as often as *sin*. In the Old Testament some form of righteousness is mentioned over five hundred times. Righteousness meant, in one sense, "right living"; in another, legal sense "right standing"; and in essence, "right being." Like anyone held to this standard, those of Jesus's time were always tired, always wrong, always bad, always unrighteous.

Was Jesus saying to them, "So you're feeling empty? Well, you just have to be more spiritual, pay closer attention to living right, and get your daily devotions going again"? Certainly not, for that would not have been anything new at all. Just the same ol' line about failure, guilt, and what not to do. So what did Jesus mean by these words? To understand, it may help to dip into a few key Scriptures.

Righteousness Remixed

In the book of Romans, Paul wrote something that would have been unconscionable for Jewish people to hear or accept: "The Gentiles, who did not pursue righteousness, have obtained it, a righteousness that is by faith; but the people of Israel, who pursued the law as the way of righteousness, have not attained their goal. Why not? Because they pursued it not by faith but as if it were by works" (Rom. 9:30–32). Paul is suggesting that the Jewish folk missed the righteousness factor and—shock and awe—the pagans actually stumbled upon it. In fact, he says many who weren't trying to be righteous were, and some who had spent their whole lives memorizing the Old Testament Scriptures and micromanaging behavior received a goose egg on the righteousness scoreboard.

Jesus is redefining what true righteousness is. Even more challenging, he's suggesting those outside the church may actually be closer to true kingdom life than many people who have been studying the Scriptures, faithfully going to church, and praying before every meal.

The word *righteousness* itself will always sound like "perfect living." But the biblical understanding of righteousness is actually based on one major truth: that is, you and I cannot be righteous . . . ever. And thus Jesus, who was perfect and holy in all ways, becomes our righteousness. We cannot make it through life without sinning, but Jesus did and died for us; thus he fulfills the righteous standard of truth for us.

Thus to hunger and thirst for righteousness doesn't mean we work harder for perfection in spiritual disciplines. Instead it means we hunger to grow into the life he modeled for us. It's a subtle difference, but important.

While in Bethlehem a year ago, I was inspired by a Lutheran pastor who had experienced incredible difficulties, both personally and in his church, during an Israeli siege of this area of the West Bank. One of our team asked him, "Why do you continue to stay in occupied Palestine to work for a peace that seems so impossible to find?" His profound answer was, "Well, the way I figure it, because of Christ's work of grace—the main job's done. Now I can focus on my hobbies, like ministry projects, and living his life as best as I can. Jesus, the Ultimate Peacemaker, did it all, so I just figure I now have a ton of free time to do things that matter to him." In other words, he was able to live without internal stress by knowing that Jesus had taken care of the big stuff. His life was simply lived in gratitude for grace, not in any huge effort to attain sainthood. The peace within sustained him as he lived in a country desperately void of peace.

Herein lies the opportunity to find real spiritual growth and deep satisfaction.

Semi-Wild at Heart

I have a friend I'll call Joe whom I nicknamed "Little Big Heart" because he's always passionate about taking over the world for God. He's a man who, for the last several years, has started men's groups all over the world using the groundbreaking book *Wild at Heart* as their premise. Written by John Eldredge, this book asserts that a man is made for an adventuresome life. For a man to find his heart, he must throw off the mundane call of the 9-to-5, strip off rote church attendance, and join the wild adventure of following Jesus.

I personally loved the book, as it tapped into my Wyatt Earp–ish desires, but I used to joke that I'd be just as happy for a "semi-wild at heart" life. One morning I showed up for one of Joe's meetings at a local Krispy Kreme joint with about eight other "wannabe wild" dudes. The night before my son,

Ryan, had endured his typical twelve hours of epileptic seizures, spaced out about every 30 to 45 minutes throughout the night, seven in all, one causing him to wet his bed. So, as I have many nights over the last seventeen years, with a sore back and glassy eyes, I carried my five-foot-nine, ninety-two-pound boy into the bathroom, pried off his soaking wet, urine-drenched Fruit of the Looms, and awkwardly lowered him into the bath to clean him up. Ryan has no strength after a grand mal seizure and is barely conscious, so after the bath I pulled him up, held him with one hand and dried him with the other, put some new clothes on him, and wrapped him in a new blanket.

On this morning, since I was already up, I staggered into the doughnut hut and found the guys reading a passage from *Wild at Heart*. I sat there dazed and confused, listening to them talk about how they were going to shake off the mundane, whittle a new spear, and head out into a dangerous new adventure with Jesus. As each man shared his dream for a fulfilled life, my turn came. All the men looked at me, and Little Big Heart said, "So, Halter, what hill are you going to take for Jesus?" After a long pause, I grabbed my maple-covered pastry in one hand, took a bite, chewed really slow so as not to miss the beauty that is a genuine Krispy Kreme, and said, "I just want a glass of milk and another doughnut, please." I sincerely was not trying to be a killjoy. I was simply enjoying my doughnut in this moment and wanted the men to know that my spiritual growth wasn't dependent upon heading out into the great unknown but was rooted in the reality of normal living.

About a year later I was in Joe's office, counseling him through a small bout of depression. Without thinking about how insensitive my question was, I looked at a huge pile of *Wild at Heart* books behind his executive desk and asked, "So what happened to your heart, man? You're not sounding all that wild anymore." He noted I was looking over his shoulder to the book pile because he swiveled around in his chair, pushed the entire stack of books off the counter, spilling his coffee, and said, "Oh, this stuff? It's crap. It doesn't work. I just don't believe you can really live an adventure with Jesus and still keep a family afloat. I barely have time to keep up with the bottom line so there's enough money for groceries right now. How am I supposed to go off on some wild adventure with God when I barely have time to mow my yard?"

As I looked at my friend, I began to pray for and over him out loud. I thanked the Lord that Joe was unwilling to settle for stale, staid religion consisting solely of church attendance and daily devotions. But I also asked God to help him find his hunger again through a faith-filled, minute-by-minute walk with God while at the same time being a stable provider for his family. After my prayer Joe said, "You know, I've always wondered how, with all the difficulty that you and Cheryl deal with, barely making it financially, and the normal overwhelming life of a pastor—you've always seemed to be the most alive dude I've known. How is that?"

I paused before saying, "I don't try to take mountains anymore. I don't have the energy for that. I have learned that Jesus is present in my mundane, day-to-day life. My spiritual growth and sense of divine adventure can be experienced anywhere—even if that 'adventure' means seeing how many times I can take care of Ryan in a typical night and still function as a semi-human the next day. I don't try to connect with God by getting away from the world or my daily realities anymore. I'm learning to find him, relate to him, learn from him, and enjoy him along the way, in the muck or joy of whatever is in front of me, just accepting what and who he drops in my path and asking him, 'Now what would you like me to do with this mess or this goodness?'"

Connecting with God along the Way

While sitting at a coffee spot in Orlando waiting for an appointment a while back, I was abruptly interrupted by the sound of a lady yelling at her husband across the street. As cars zoomed by, I watched as she riddled the man with accusations about an apparent affair she had caught him in. Through the loud sounds of cars and trucks whizzing by, I was still held captive by the colorful language the lady was using and found it impossible to look away—until, that is, I heard another woman a little closer to me, standing at the nearest street corner screaming at her two children who had almost been hit by a car as they strolled into the crosswalk. Like fans at Wimbledon, my head swiveled back and forth between the two dramas.

Then, as if I were taking off 3-D glasses, my vision panned back to the spot where I was standing. I was on a Starbucks outdoor patio and had been viewing the twin dramas through a thick hedge of dogwood tree branches. While the two screaming sessions continued, I started to realize that I had been watching these unsettling events through a screen of beauty. I actually reached out and felt one of the tree limbs, a symbol of peace, calm, and beauty. Each branch had bright green buds and small pink flowers in the beginning stages of bloom. Strangely, I stopped hearing the dramas and thanked God for the tree, his peace, and the blessing of my peaceful relationship with my wife and kids.

In later reflection, the lesson I came away with was this: we can choose our focus in spite of all that is happening around us. My ability to switch my focus to God's peace rather than the turmoil that is always brewing somewhere in life is ever available. It's up to me to tune in to it. Sometimes "wild adventure" comes simply by embracing interruption, a willingness to stop and listen to someone without hurrying off to the next appointment. Sometimes it's a quiet act of service that lightens a friend's burdens or celebrating a win with a buddy who's been lapping from the trough of hard luck. Most often, at least in my world where my best-laid "wild man" plans are constantly interrupted by the next family or church crisis at hand, peace and adventure come in accepting whatever comes at me next, taking one event, person, problem, or celebration at a time.

It's spiritual formation *along the way*, and it's *seeing Jesus through all the minutia of temporal existence.*

Connecting with God, Uniquely

Not too long ago a mentor of mine named Paul asked if he could do one of those long and involved personal assessments on me. I was struggling with my life's calling and my gifting and wondering where to focus my limited energy. As he pored over an eighty-page printout of graphs and charts about me, he looked up and said, "Wow, Halter, you're an aesthetic."

"You mean, like a monk?" I asked. "I think this test might be goofy, because the last thing I could ever do is live the life of a cloistered saint."

Paul laughed and said, "You're thinking of the word *ascetic*. You are an *aesthetic*, which means you connect with God through all your senses."

I paused and stroked my chin. "That sounds sort of attractive."

Paul smiled and continued, "I bet when you are on your Harley with the wind blowing through your arm hairs, or out golfing, or walking around that little park lake by your house, or sitting in a Starbucks with music, a warm mug of coffee, and inviting décor—pleasing sound, taste, touch, and sights— you probably connect with God pretty naturally, don't you?"

As he spoke, something in me resonated so deeply it is still hard to describe in words. It felt like finding home. It felt as if someone had lifted a two-ton yoke off my neck and a fresh, free air was blowing within. I could hardly contain my excitement. "Paul, I can't even pray sitting down! I can't study Scripture in quiet. I have to be moving to really hear anything! Is that what you're talking about?"

He grinned. "Keep talking."

"Okay, when I'm helping someone in a hands-on way or enjoying a great conversation with someone, I feel more alive spiritually than when I'm singing in the church I pastor. Are you telling me that this qualifies as a spiritual life?"

"Absolutely, positively. It's how God relates to you, it's how you hear him most clearly, and it's how you live out your calling most naturally. For you, that's spirituality at its best and healthiest."

Connecting with God through Eating and Drinking

Contrast the above with this: "Hugh, I believe you have a keen sense of being called to ministry, and I'm sure God will direct you someday, but your seeming lack of interest and inability to hear from God during our exercises is beginning to distract the rest of the class. I'd suggest you drop this course and pick up something else."

These words were from my professor of "contemplative spirituality." This class focused on teaching us to practice the spiritual discipline of silence and listening. In every class the prof would send us off to the library or cubicles around the building where we were told to "empty your mind, focus on nothing, use repetitive chants to focus, and then listen to what God is telling you." The last thirty minutes of class were reserved for group sharing, where we were expected to let the other meditators know what God told us. I'm an honest guy, so from week one to week six I'd answer truthfully, "Nope, didn't hear anything again, just found myself struggling to think about nothing."

Whenever I have tried to understand or enter into standardized forms of spiritual formation or discipline, I have been let down. Whether it was praying at a cubicle, memorizing Navigator Scripture cards (a method of Bible memory whereby one carries around business cards with verses on them), fasting, or singing in church, they all left me bored and using a credit card to pick yesterday's beef jerky out of my teeth. Well-meaning mentors have taken me to monasteries with them, but after an hour I'm walking down to the friars' beer and bread shop for a little snack. I was even assigned a monk as my personal spiritual guide, but he reminded me of a kid I beat up in the sixth grade, so I just couldn't lock in to the vesper way.

These experiences and a handful of others made me question my calling and level of spirituality. However, I'm learning that Jesus not only understands, he has made a way for blokes like me and maybe you.

In Luke 5 some spiritual formation gurus say to Jesus, "John's disciples often fast and pray, and so do the disciples of the Pharisees, but yours go on eating and drinking" (v. 33). In other words, "Jesus, any spiritually serious person focuses on spiritual disciplines, but the dudes who call you rabbi hardly ever participate in these traditional activities. What gives?"

The beauty and freedom of Jesus's response is profound. He makes it clear that fasting is not always necessary or even preferred. Though spiritual "disciplines" have their place, especially for contemplative personality types, Jesus grows us in hundreds of ways. Especially for those of us who are wired for action, Jesus will grow us as we're on the go with him.

None of us, no matter our personality type, will grow in some ways unless we're active, challenged, in new environments, out in the streets, and in community with others who are also actively following him. Yes, you can pick up a few tidbits of helpful information in a church service, and you get encouraged in a small group, but the "devotional life" Jesus demonstrated happened in strange places with people we would think of as out of our comfort zones. To Jesus, spiritual formation isn't solely cognitive. It's visceral. It includes and can be helped by classic practices, but it will only grow exponentially when you are involved with real people in significant conversations and life experiences. Spiritual formation is not passive or hermit-like; it is out there, engaging the culture.

Making His Kingdom Tangible to You

Last year I helped create a workbook called *The Tangible Kingdom Primer*, in large part to help people find a wider way to experience spiritual formation using all of their senses. Although I'm not personally big on journaling, we've found that providing an experiential pathway for discovering the kingdom life—or in other words, helping make God's kingdom tangible—seems to open up a new world to the religiously weary.

The fourth day of each week in the workbook is what we call an action day, where we encourage the reader to go beyond considering a concept about Jesus and actually try his way of life. All of these prompts are intended to activate a sensory-level experience so that folks can hear and know and feel God via a wider variety of ways than the standard one or two that are most emphasized and taught.

Most of the emails I get are from people who have experienced deep change during these days. The first week we ask people to act cross-culturally, like missionaries, and do two silly things. One is to cross their street, and another is to cross their fence. Here's one email from George, who happens to be a pastor:

> Hugh, you don't know me, but I have been a pastor for thirty years and have to thank you for helping me, after all these years, finally experience God. In the first week of your *Tangible Kingdom Primer*, you suggested that we cross our street and then cross our fence to relate with people. At first glance, it sounded too simple, but here's what happened. While looking out my window, I saw my neighbor at his mailbox. I have known him for fifteen years. I wave at him, we occasionally exchange pleasantries, but I've never really approached him with the hopes of becoming a friend. I was shocked at how resistant I was, even insecure to go outside and get my mail while he did. I actually wimped out.
>
> The next day I decided to go walk around the block to meet the man on the other side of my fence. As I rounded

the corner, all of sudden I realized that I had interacted with him once. Six years ago we got in an argument because I cut down a limb of his tree that was encroaching on my side of the fence. Again, I was paralyzed with the realization that to actually engage him, I'd have to ask forgiveness for my harsh words. This time I forced myself to his front door, rang the bell, and came clean. We shook hands, and he invited me in for coffee. I walked home absolutely changed and realized that this was the most spiritually formative thirty minutes I'd had in thirty years in the pastorate. Thanks!

Jesus wanted to grow average people into revolutionaries, housewives into leaders, businessmen into priests, teenagers into missionaries, and artists into cultural architects of kingdom work. To do this, he took his learners on boats in heavy seas and into the back alleys with prostitutes, beggars, and thieves. He walked them to the top of mountains, into beautiful gardens, along the seashores, and into the dark catacombs underneath Jerusalem. He had them look at and touch flowers, watch birds, and consider strange riddles and stories told by campfires. He woke them up early and made them stay up late; he forced them to do things beyond their comfort level and befriend people they never would have reached out to without his encouragement. He included them in real-life dramas with the sick, the outcasts, the demonized, the abused, and the sinners in every depth of dysfunction. It was all to help them stretch, to grow more like the God he'd been telling them about. Yes, on rare occasion he took them into the synagogue and had some intimate devotional time with them, and even asked them to pray with him. But the vast majority of his time was spent taking whatever or whoever happened to show up in his path and using it as an opportunity to bring a heavenly lesson down to earthly people.

So what if true, holistic spiritual growth only happens as and if we go with Jesus? That sort of changes everything, doesn't it?

If you've ever felt spiritually hungry, perhaps this might help you understand why. If you've bonked when trying to relate to God, maybe it's because you've tried to fill this hunger and thirst with religion, church attendance, "devotions," and going to small groups—where you talk more about religion and church and how to fill yourself with more Scripture. If so, consider developing an appetite for a little less talk and a lot more action.

Think of your natural giftings and match them with a need in front of you. Help a widow with her yard; be an extra "uncle" to a kid without a dad; ask your neighbor over for beer, burgers on the grill, and good conversation. And along the way, you may start to experience a spiritual satisfaction that quenches your thirst for meaning.

A Lesson from Jillian

On a coffee table in our living room is a book by Jillian Michaels titled *Making the Cut*. Jillian is one of the drill sergeant fitness gurus on the popular TV show *The Biggest Loser*. In the book she, like my spiritual mentor, says there's not one way for everyone to lose weight and that each person has a different body type, muscle makeup, and appetite. Some people are satisfied through celery, legumes, and iced tea; others, like me, are satisfied with beef followed by a stick of butter with a bacon chaser and then working it off by mountain biking my butt off, literally.

It's not only okay, it's really important to find God in your own way and experience a sense of spiritual growth and satisfaction along the way of normal life. Some will experience God by simple acts of kindness to others; some through being in nature; some through quiet times of reflection on Scripture; and others while being with those in the midst of their own struggles. Some will hear from God in a church service, and others will sense God's voice while having a cup of coffee with some friends. We've so greatly limited God, and because of this, we have limited people's ability to come alive in his presence—each in the way that they hear and serve God best.

 To consider: When you look back to times when you came alive spiritually, what were you doing? Were you in a more contemplative, quiet place, or were you more active? Try to figure out where God tends to meet with you the most easily.

 To do: Pray while walking this week. Go somewhere that will force you to look at people's faces while you talk to God. The reality is that 60 percent of the people you see will be from a broken home, one third of all the women will have been sexually abused, most people will be under financial stress, one third don't have a father, and 10 percent will be living in poverty and not know where the next meal comes from. See if the intensity of your prayers and spiritual life takes a turn upward.

"It is better to think of church in the ale-house than to think of the ale-house in church."

Martin Luther

8

SIN IN THE PERIPHERY

Leaving Judgmentalism in the Rearview Mirror

Blessed are the merciful,
   for they will be shown mercy.
                Matthew 5:7

My day of reckoning had arrived. It was a Tuesday morning near the end of December, a date I had been dreading for several months. I was sitting in a packed courtroom in downtown Denver. Normally I would have been in our district courthouse, but the main office, I recall the officer saying, was for "the more serious traffic infractions." A few weeks before, after church (why is it always after church?), I was speeding home because my son had left a message on my cell saying, "Dad, I feel like I'm going to have a seizure." Cheryl was gone, so I was making haste down a main drag through metro Denver.

Blue lights, an angry officer, and then, to my shock, I was handed a traffic ticket displaying my speed as 90 miles per hour! Gulp. My wife and kids are accustomed to me getting stopped by the police for a variety of minor infractions, mostly for going a wee bit over the posted limit. In fact, it's happened so much over the course of our lives that my children don't even say anything when I get pulled over. They normally just roll their eyes in my rearview mirror while they keep listening to their iPods. Call me perceptive, but I doubted my wife, Cheryl, who takes much of my ADD-like behavior in stride, was going to overlook the fact that I was going *twice* the legal speed limit! I know a pastor should never lie, but I thought the wrath of my wife would actually be worse than the wrath of God on this one, so I kept my mouth shut and didn't tell her about it.

On the dreaded morning, without telling Cheryl, I got in my car and drove downtown, hoping my million-dollar fine would be no more painful than, say, a root canal.

After a large bailiff asked us all to rise and respect the Honorable Judge Wilcox, we were allowed to be seated. At this point the stern-looking judge said, "Thank you all for showing up today. If you would all look at your ticket, you'll notice that some of yours are yellow. This means that you will not need an attorney, and after I give you a fine, you can simply pay it here and be on your way." I looked down and with rising alarm noted my ticket was not yellow but a bright, ominous red. He continued, "If you have a red ticket, it means you may need an attorney, and if you can't afford one, the court will issue you one."

Uh-oh, I thought, *this a tad more serious than I realized.* Visions of my poor pastorly self sitting behind bars played in my mind. I imagined having to ask my ministry wingman Matt to bail me out of the slammer, then pondered how

I'd explain this situation to my wife, our staff, our church, and my teenage daughters. Just as the panic reached heart-palpitating level, the judge said, "So let's begin. Hugh Halter, can you please step up to the microphone?" That's right, out of three hundred glassy-eyed could-be criminals, I was the first one called. I rose on shaky legs and headed toward the microphone like a condemned man to the guillotine.

"Sir," the judge said, "I hope you didn't get an attorney."

Oh, great, I thought. *My crime is so great that it's beyond an attorney's ability to help.* Maybe the paddy wagon was waiting for me in the back, ready to whisk me off to the pokey.

I swallowed and found my voice. "No, sir, I do not have an attorney."

"Well, that's good, Mr. Halter, because apparently, we've lost all the paperwork on your file, so you are free to go. Merry Christmas!"

I stood in stunned amazement, fighting down the urge to jump over the bailiff and kiss the judge on the lips, when a large African American lady stood up, raised her hands as if lifting the roof, and said, "Oh, yeah. The Lord is on your side, sweetie!" Then the place erupted with applause. Seriously, it was like a sappy scene from every feel-good Christmas movie ever made. People behind me were high-fiving each other. There was laughter and well wishes. I half expected to hear a bell sound as an angel got his wings. I grinned gratefully and quickly slipped away before anyone in authority could change their mind.

I got in my car, took a deep breath, and thanked God that on this one miraculous morning, mercy had trumped justice.

Mercy or Justice? You Pick

If you had to choose between a world where *mercy* always wins or *justice* always wins, what would you choose? If you pick justice, no one ever gets off scot-free; no one gets an unfair advantage; no one gets away with bad behavior, abuse, or being a jerk. Punishment is always swift and appropriate; black-and-white judgment wins every time. Sounds like a pretty good world, doesn't it? If you're tired of seeing political wrangling, earmarks for self-interest groups, and partisan pandering; if you can't stand hearing about any more child abductions, sex abuse, Ponzi schemes, philandering athletes, pedophile priests, or narcissistic celebrities, a world of justice may be just what the doctor ordered.

My guess is that most would pick justice for several reasons. First, when we compare our own behavioral flaws to others', we tend to come out smelling pretty good. Second, most of us actually enjoy seeing the bad guys get their comeuppance. Third, we fear a world of mercy because we assume most who receive it will abuse it.

It's no wonder that the world to which Jesus came struggled with the concept of merciful grace. Every culture has its own code of ethics, and the Romans, Greeks, and Jews all held to the rule of justice. Roman values centered around courage, restraint, duty, and truth. Greeks valued wisdom, constraint, and physical strength. In their mind mercy was considered weakness. The Jewish people lived by the law of Moses, the Ten Commandments, Levitical laws, and the myriad rules for holiness that were added later. If there had been bumper stickers for camels back then, "An eye for an eye!" might have been a popular slogan. Retaliation was considered holy, so swift punishment was doled out for any and all sins. You faced stoning for immorality, blasphemy, stealing, or working on the Sabbath. If you were sick, barren, suffering from leprosy, or in your menstrual cycle, you faced social separation. "Unclean" was a term thrown around as often as we might say "gross," "stupid," or "moronic." Essentially, anyone struggling with life's hard issues—be it the homeless, the mentally ill, the immoral, or the financially unstable—was judged as receiving whatever misery they deserved.

Although I'm sure there were times tenderhearted citizens must have felt the punishments were a bit harsh for the crimes, they did not dare ask for grace. Mercy just didn't compute with the current cultural theology or brand of social justice. Thus sin or "sins" were the primary lens through which people observed one another. If you sin, you're out. Sin big, you're really out. In fact, you are probably dead.

Blockhead Christianity

Focusing on sin is a natural tendency when you grow up in what some sociologists call a "bounded set" worldview. A bounded set is like a square box that consists of doctrines, behavioral expectations, traditions, and organizational or social patterns. These edges create a bounded set of lines designating who is in or out and also what it takes to be in or out. This type of arrangement is like when a farmer erects a fence to keep his own animals inside and safe while also keeping out the bad things like wolves, foxes, and thieves. Although a bounded set can have positive aspects, within the religious or church world, it tends to make us "blockheaded" and divert us away from mercy.

The Ten Commandments, for example, represented a bounded set—ten rules God's people held as a plumb line for a good life. To stay within was actually healthy for the people, but as the interpretation of the commandments became more legalistic, and as other rules or lines were added and smaller boxes were created inside the bigger box, judgment on sin and on sinners themselves became prolific. In a bounded set, mercy is hard to find because the lines are black and white. This is why in the book of Hebrews, four entire chapters are given to explaining why the law (a bounded set) is made obsolete by Christ's payment. A new or better way is now available. No more boxed-in religion or blockheaded Christians!

Circles Are Better Than Lines

When my friend Greg helps young couples get ready for marriage, he sits them down and draws two diagrams. The first diagram is just a line in the middle of a piece of paper. Then he explains that this line represents trouble. Many if not most marriages operate on a "line system," and it goes like this: "We'll get along fine as long as you stay on my side of the line or come over to my side whenever we disagree."

On another piece of paper he draws a circle and explains that this type of marriage is one where one spouse says to the other, "I married the whole circle of who you are. Inside the circle are all sorts of things I love and like about you. But I also know that inside the circle are some behaviors and ways of thinking that I personally do not like. Still, on our wedding day I chose to marry everything inside the circle. And if these things never change, I'll still accept the entire circle and care for the entire circle that is you. I'm committed to and love the whole you."

The "circle marriages" would be more like what sociologists call a "centered set." A centered set draws people to the middle by wooing them with something they want. A good buddy of mine from Australia was speaking to pastors and shared how cattle ranchers who own thousands of acres would never dream of trying to fence in all their outback land. It would be simply impossible; they could never maintain it all, and eventually the dividing lines would be compromised anyway. So what do they do? Simple. Instead of building fences, they build really good watering holes. They know that at the center of every cow's basic needs is a thirst for water. In terrain where drought is sure and water is scarce, if you build a well, trust me, the cows will come. In cow-speak, Jesus was the well, and people tended to be irresistibly drawn to him, especially those who had been abused by legalistic blockheads. If we are going to be apprentices of Jesus, we're going to have to trade in our boxes and lines for circles.

You may remember I'm writing this while my daughter Alli is sixteen. Since she was twelve months old she's been pushing against lines and walls. When she got tired of waking up inside a crib with wooden bars holding her in, what did my little "don't fence me in" daughter do? She climbed out, flipped over, and cracked her arm (the first of many more broken bones and trips to the emergency room to come).

I know some of you must be thinking, *See, Halter? That's a perfect example of why we need to have fences and walls and why it's good to pressure people to live according to God's holy standards. It's for their own safety and protection.*

I grant that you have a few points. After all, when God gave Moses the Ten Commandments, he said, "Hey, listen up! Obey these things, because if you do, it will go well with you." But there is one little problem: the system didn't work any better then than it does now. Israelites were no better at staying in the walls than Americans are today. They kept climbing out, busting their arms, being put back in, and eventually climbing out and busting their arms again . . . over and over. In other words, they kept sinning.

The aforementioned Greg (of the line and circle illustration) is also the one I called when I was freaking out about how to keep my daughter fenced in. Mind you, this daughter now carries car keys that operate a vehicle that can carry her to homes with boys who want to do things boys want to do and to places where other kids like to smoke things and drink things and try things that fill my head with panic.

"So," I asked Greg, "how do I rein her in? How do I keep her from screwing up her life?"

Greg smiled compassionately. "You can't."

Not the answer I was hoping for. But he continued with something along the lines of, "You can only hope that you have dug a few inviting and welcoming wells of God's ways, so that she always knows where to come back to when she's thirsty for things that are good, and pure, and right, and desirable."

nnot tell you how much easier it is for me to pontificate the line and circle theory and the bounded set versus centered set philosophy when it comes to the church than it is to apply these to the teen-turning-into-adult who lives in my house. But before I wilted in despair, Greg went on to explain, "There's a dynamic of personal maturity, a state of independence that all kids come to at some point in their life. Some kids don't get there until they're twenty-eight, and some get there at age fourteen. It's when they are ready and insistent upon making their own choices for their life. Of course, you have some control over when you put up appropriate guardrails for them, but as they age, choose your battles carefully. The ultimate goal is for our kids to know God and choose wisely, intrinsically, from their own free will. And to get there, they've got to be allowed some freedom to choose and fail. That means as they get older and take ownership over their own faith, mercy becomes critical."

Alli expressed in no uncertain terms her independence along with her desire to exert her will at a younger age than I was ready to accept. Greg taught me that when the switch of independence hits, behavior and faith (fences) are not nearly as important as relationship. An open, loving, honest, vulnerable, accepting relationship with our kids, Greg explained, is the well that draws our teens to us and hopefully, eventually, to the God we love. He said, "It's all about relationship. Keep it open. Keep them coming back to talk and get loved on and listened to and valued." Essentially Greg was teaching me what Jesus is trying to teach us.

Behavior Management Is a Pig's Trough

Now, I will admit, my initial reaction to Greg's response was, "This is crap, dude! Are you saying I just have to let my daughter make lousy decisions?" My friend smiled, then took me to a Scripture. (I hate that.) The passage is well known: the parable of the prodigal son in Luke 15. You can read it yourself, but essentially the story opens with a son who decides to get outside the box and cross the line of good behavior. He grabs his dad's inheritance and becomes a Hebrew Gone Wild. He blows all his dough on sin and debauchery, goes broke, and ends up eating scraps alongside the local pigs, who, by the way, were probably living in a pen. Sin eventually reveals itself as its own fenced-in system.

Well, the son gets desperate and heads back to the father (the center or "well" of his life). To the son's amazement, his dad is standing on the porch looking for him, and when he sees his beat-up kid coming up the road, he runs to him, invites him back in, throws him a huge party, and celebrates that his son has returned.

Meanwhile, his bounded-set, justice-oriented older brother—you know, the one who stayed inside the "bounds" of his dad's farm and behaved well—gets a little judgmental. He goes pouting to Daddy and says, "I stayed inside the box. I didn't sin like that little punk. I do all the things you ask me to, and I avoid the things you don't want me to do, but you showed the little guy grace, accepted him back in, and threw him a huge party. So what am I missing here? I don't get it."

And Dad (a Jesus figure) replies, "Son, I've always provided this well of goodness for both of you, and you've benefited hugely from all I've given. Your brother left, tasted the bitterness of life outside my center, and came back. That's how it is supposed to work. You both get all this through me and being in relationship with me." One is left to wonder if the elder brother ever drinks deeply of the relationship with his father or just stays in the house, the way some Christians stay near the church but miss out on a living friendship with the Father.

Well, Greg had me. God leads with relationship, and in the context of that friendship our behaviors naturally change and we allow one another freedom to take custody of our own faith.

141

James 2:13 says, "Mercy triumphs over judgment." It's a whole new bumper sticker! If we want to be like Jesus, we'll live more like the father of the prodigal and less like a courtroom judge.

Sacrilege and Sin

We have gone quite a distance now into Jesus's sacrilegious ways, and I assume you're starting to see some new spiritual viewpoints, or at least get that Jesus looks at life, God, and humanity much differently than we tend to see things. If you were sitting on the hill listening to Jesus give the Sermon on the Mount, about now you'd either be scratching your head wondering why you brought the whole family out to hear this crackpot or looking down, digging a twig into the dirt, processing every syllable he uttered.

This "mercy trumping justice" concept would have been the antithesis of everything you'd ever heard. But would it have sounded intriguing? *Does* it sound intriguing? What would being an apprentice of Jesus require of me if I were to take this viewpoint seriously? Would viewing the world through eyes of radical grace in some way feel like abandoning my solid faith in God and his standards?

These are all the questions we now have to dive into, because to live by the relational law of mercy over the black-and-white law of Moses (sin management), we will have to get used to doing something really strange. We will have to overlook *sin*, or at least not make as big a deal of it as we have in the past. This is the power of mercy.

Jesus Was Not Freaked Out by Sinners

Sin is mentioned over 1,300 times throughout Scripture. Without a doubt, sin was the central lens through which religious types viewed everything. Sin, sinfulness, sinning, and sinners was the pair of glasses you would have put on every morning. Through these glasses you'd figure out how you compared to others on the "sin-o-meter." Sin was the basis on which you explained to your children why someone else was sick or poor, lame or blind, deserving the praise or judgment of other townspeople. This sin-centered worldview was used to justify withholding practical help from some in need, and it was the basis for all social and religious separation. This is why it is remarkable that Jesus looked past sin as if it wasn't his biggest concern. Let me give you a few examples, starting with Mark 2:15–17:

> While Jesus was having dinner at Levi's house, many tax collectors and sinners were eating with him and his disciples, for there were many who followed him. When the teachers of the law who were Pharisees saw him eating with the sinners and tax collectors, they asked his disciples: "Why does he eat with tax collectors and sinners?" On hearing this, Jesus said to them, "It is not the healthy who need a doctor, but the sick. I have not come to call the righteous, but sinners."

The scandalous issue in this passage is that Jesus ate with the types of people that the religious folks viewed as sinful. Eating together back then was much more than just grabbing a burger on an unleavened bun. To sup with someone meant you accepted them as a part of your circle of friends. To share food or wine was to acknowledge to everyone that the folks you were dining with were "in" with you. Therefore, Jesus's willingness to enjoy a meal with the "unsanctioned" made a loud statement: sinners were accepted and enjoyed as his companions and friends.

"But aren't there Scriptures about not eating with immoral people?" you may ask. Yes, Paul speaks to that issue—but he's not referring to the outsiders. He's referring to the insiders. Read 1 Corinthians 5:9–11:

> I wrote to you in my letter not to associate with sexually immoral people—not at all meaning the people of this world

who are immoral, or the greedy and swindlers, or idolaters. In that case you would have to leave this world. But now I am writing you that you must not associate with anyone who claims to be a brother or sister but is sexually immoral or greedy, an idolater or a slanderer, a drunkard or swindler. Do not even eat with such people.

The point is clear in context. A person who called himself a Christian was participating in egregious sexual sin. This is a clear example of how we should hold those inside the camp to holiness and challenge their blatant, "in your face" sinful lifestyle choices, even to the point where we would have to say, "Yo, Bill, your total unwillingness to see your choices as hurtful to this Christian community leaves me no other choice but to ask you to take some time away from the community until you can come to your senses and quit making us look bad."

But it's also equally clear that Paul is not asking us to take the same position with those who are not enlightened to the way of God. Sinners are to be accepted at face value.

In John 9, Jesus blows apart the bounded set philosophy a little more:

They brought to the Pharisees the man who had been blind. Now the day on which Jesus had made the mud and opened the man's eyes was a Sabbath. Therefore the Pharisees also asked him how he had received his sight. "He put mud on my eyes," the man replied, "and I washed, and now I see."

Some of the Pharisees said, "This man is not from God, for he does not keep the Sabbath."

But others asked, "How can a sinner perform such signs?" So they were divided. (vv. 13–16)

The Pharisees in many ways were experts at bounded set religion. When someone failed to meet even just one small aspect of their "standards," the Pharisees wrote them off as being without merit. In this case, ironically, they dismissed the miracle of the blind man's healing because Jesus did it on the Sabbath, and according to the letter of their law, no "work"—including miracles—could be performed on that holy day. Talk about an exercise in missing the point. Here's more of the story:

> Then they turned again to the blind man, "What have you to say about him? It was your eyes he opened."
>
> The man replied, "He is a prophet."
>
> They still did not believe that he had been blind and had received his sight until they sent for the man's parents. "Is this your son?" they asked. "Is this the one you say was born blind? How is it that now he can see?"
>
> "We know he is our son," the parents answered, "and we know he was born blind. But how he can see now, or who opened his eyes, we don't know. Ask him. He is of age; he will speak for himself." His parents said this because they were afraid of the Jewish leaders, who already had decided that anyone who acknowledged that Jesus was the Messiah would be put out of the synagogue. (vv. 17–22)

Here we also see how many people, stuck inside their self-constructed boxes, are afraid to be considered on the outs. These parents must have been thrilled when their son experienced the healing of his sight, not only for him but also because this healing would remove the stigma of sin over their family. Healthy children meant that God was blessing a family because of their righteousness. Isn't it interesting, then, that the parents were afraid that if they acknowledged the Healer, they would be "put out" of the synagogue? In fact, it appears fear of rejection by the "insiders" trumped their joy over their son's healing:

> That was why his parents said, "He is of age; ask him."
>
> A second time they summoned the man who had been blind. "Give glory to God by telling the truth," they said. "We know this man is a sinner."

He replied, "Whether he is a sinner or not, I don't know. One thing I do know. I was blind but now I see!"

Then they asked him, "What did he do to you? How did he open your eyes?"

He answered, "I have told you already and you did not listen. Why do you want to hear it again? Do you want to become his disciples too?"

Then they hurled insults at him and said, "You are this fellow's disciple! We are disciples of Moses! We know that God spoke to Moses, but as for this fellow, we don't even know where he comes from." (vv. 23–28)

Here again you see how people prefer to live life by the law of Moses in a black-and-white mind-set. What's funny is how this young man, with tongue in cheek, says, "Hey, you'd better stop asking me the same dumb questions, because if I keep answering the same way, you too may end up being a disciple of this guy and following his out-of-the-box thinking!"

The man answered, "Now that is remarkable! You don't know where he comes from, yet he opened my eyes. We know that God does not listen to sinners. He listens to the godly person who does his will. Nobody has ever heard of opening the eyes of a man born blind. If this man were not from God, he could do nothing."

To this they replied, "You were steeped in sin at birth; how dare you lecture us!" And they threw him out. (vv. 30–34)

I can't help but picture this guy, who sees clearly now in more ways than one, smiling at the ridiculousness of the Pharisees, then nodding gratefully toward Jesus and walking away to take in the scenery.

Sinners Really Do Love Jesus

Mary poured perfume on Jesus's feet while he was eating with a Jewish priest. Some scholars believe she was a prostitute.

Apparently, the perfume cost her half a year's wages. Judas, who would later betray Jesus, tried to stop her display of adoration using the ol' "we could feed a lot of poor people" argument—more to impress the religious muckety-mucks than out of any real feeling of sorrow for the plight of the poor. Not only was the perfumed oil expensive, it was what the woman used to make herself smell attractive so she could turn tricks every night as a local hooker, so the money she was pouring out was actually gained from her morally impure job. But Jesus, sensitively and appreciatively, allowed her to pour her "wages of sin" all over his feet.

Sacrilege! I love it.

I remember once that an elder of my church told me we should not accept money from a man who drove a beer truck for a local microbrewery. He said it was "unclean" money and God would judge us for not asking this man to quit his job and find more wholesome employment. I told him that making money from the production and distribution of malted hops and barley (better known as beer) was the trade of choice for many monastic communities over the centuries, but that just made him drool with anger. The beer truck driver was a man wanting to give what he had to a place where he'd found love and acceptance. To lecture him on the sinfulness of his "dirty money" would wound him for doing something good and put up a mile-high fence between us. If I had followed the elder's advice, I would not have seen this man in our church again. The relationship with this man meant more to me than any religion-based controversy about the appropriateness of his income source.

So why do you think Jesus overlooks so much sin and sin byproducts? It's simple but profound: he took care of sin for us. Done, finished! And what remains? Relationship. Because he managed the sin of the whole world, we no longer need to micromanage sin in ourselves or other people. Sin is still a huge deal, and Jesus still hates to see what sin does to our lives. But like a loving parent running through an oncoming crowd of faceless people in a New York subway station, desperately looking for their lost son or daughter, Jesus looks past our outward condition and pursues the renovation of our hearts. Likewise, when a lost son or daughter finds themselves being scooped up and rescued from sin's lostness, they want to acknowledge their sin and change their behavior.

The final story I want to share is that of a woman who was violently brought out into the public square in order to test Jesus's theology (see John 8:2–11). It is a classic example of the main point of this chapter: mercy trumps judgment. The woman had been caught in adultery. According to the law of Moses, this woman must die by stoning. This time Jesus adds a parameter to their sin punishment system by saying, "Go ahead and throw some stones, as long as you haven't sinned either—ever!" That wasn't the response the authorities were expecting. In their minds, there were big sins and little sins and medium sins—sins worthy of death, sins that required you to sacrifice a sheep, some just a bird, and some for which you paid a little money to the temple. In this story Jesus tells the woman, "I don't condemn you." The Pharisees were so smug in their assurance that they'd not committed her particular "gigantic" sin, they were thrown off guard by the fact that Jesus apparently didn't distinguish between small sins and the super-sized variety.

Though we all continue to rebel against this merciful truth, sin was paid for, covered, and managed by Jesus. All kinds of sin. So we no longer need to micromanage, sort, and categorize sin. The whole of it has been taken care of, paid in full.

Hebrews 7:27 says it concisely: "Unlike the other high priests, he does not need to offer sacrifices day after day, first for his own sins, and then for the sins of the people. He sacrificed for their sins once for all when he offered himself."

Because of Christ's payment for our sin, our faith is no longer about sin management. It's a faith system based on grace. No longer are we to navel gaze and micromanage morality. We instead can live life to the fullest and learn to navigate the vices of our flesh with our bigger desire to please our Savior. No more fear of a God who stiff-arms us until we get it all right. He's taken care of sin. We're good. And because of that, we can relax and sleep peacefully. This fact is what ultimately sets us free to live without judgment upon others. We don't have to sin-manage their lives, nor teach them to toe the line to a set of behaviors they need to obey *before* they come to faith. We can now be kind like Jesus, for it's the kindness of God that leads to repentance (see Rom. 2:4).

Apprenticing Nonjudgment

A missions agency I used to work with had a one-year communal living apprenticeship process. The goal of the year was to create a culturally savvy missionary, able to dive deep into the lives of those coping without God. How did they train them? There were many great training sessions, but one stood out to me. One evening they blindfolded a would-be missionary, sat him in a chair in a dark barn, and positioned the other participants around him. One of the participants was to be a voice that advocated for the blindfolded missionary. This advocate's purpose was to speak the words of God, read Scripture, and say things that would be considered "wholesome to the soul." Everyone else was there to swear, curse, and say anything that might distract the missionary from hearing God's voice.

The point of this "spiritual hazing" exercise is clear. The trainers are trying to teach the leader to be able to look past the sin and sinners and stay focused on the truth of their own belovedness to God and, therefore, how much God loves even those hurling insults in their direction. This is a critical skill that I believe every apprentice of Jesus must take seriously. We have to stop flinching or gasping for air every time someone swears, has too much to drink, or rides their bike naked through the city square during a gay pride parade.

I know I'm weird, but since I have accepted how much of my sin Jesus has overlooked, I now have mercy when I see other people sin. It's like a parent watching their three-year-old picking their nose and wiping it on the seat of their car. Yes, you wish they had the maturity to understand how inappropriate this is, but you don't kick them out of the car!

So what are we to do with sinners? It is common to hear, "Judge the sin, not the sinner." I believe that because mercy trumps judgment, Jesus would say, "Don't judge the sin or the sinner." Just overlook the sin until Jesus has their heart; he'll take care of the sinner and the sin.

In truth, the way we can love all the wildly sinning prodigals around us is to realize that we are prodigals too. As we let ourselves be loved and known by the Father, patiently loving and showing mercy to others who are having their turn at the pig slop becomes much, much easier. It becomes less a special gift we bestow now and again on the truly repentant and more like an entirely new way of seeing.

 To consider: Have you been holding any grudges against or severed your relationship with anyone who didn't come to your side of "the line"? How might you show mercy and restore this relationship?

 To do: Forgive a debt that someone owes you. Call them and let them know that they are no longer bound by the original agreement. In so doing, you will be identifying with what Christ does for you all the time.

"Be a sinner and sin strongly, but more strongly have faith and rejoice in Christ."

Martin Luther

150

9

JESUS ON A JOHN DEERE

Bulldozing Boundaries to Daddy's Dinner

Blessed are the pure in heart,
for they will see God.

Matthew 5:8

H ere are two questions that could change your life.

First, does God love everyone? If you answered yes, you are a winner.

Second, does God like everyone? If you answered yes, you should reread the Bible.

The Scriptures indicate that God allows the rain to fall on the just and the unjust, so we know he doesn't play favorites, but apparently he does *have* favorites.

David was "a man after God's own heart" (see Acts 13:22). Here's a guy who slept with another man's wife, then killed the husband, but God still liked the guy!

"And Enoch walked with God" (Gen. 5:24 NKJV). Now that's pretty cool. As busy as God was, something about Enoch caused God to literally want to take a manly stroll with him.

"Noah, at least you're a righteous man, so because of you, I'll spare the universe" (see Gen. 7:1).

Then there was the head-scratcher, Rahab. She was a woman who slept with a different man every night, maybe two or three. God, however, spared her entire family from the destruction of Jericho, and she made the Hebrews hall of fame—a picture of faith and good works (see Heb. 11:31).

Apparently God does fancy a certain kind of human. Yes, he does love everyone, he died for everyone, and he allows the natural pain of life to touch us all, but evidently there's a type of person who seems to capture God's heart, a type of person whose picture ends up on God's refrigerator. What is the one characteristic that seems to set all these people apart?

Being pure in heart. What does it mean to be pure in heart? I think I'd rather lead here with an illustration rather than a definition.

I've written a few stories about my son Ryan because our lives often revolve around his epilepsy. Everyone likes him, but because of his severe disability, he hasn't had too many real friends he can call his own. That is, until he met a guy I'll call Tony. To others, Tony is a young man who has been in and out of trouble with the law, made a lot of bad decisions, had trouble controlling his temper and his alcohol consumption, and often made messes of the relationships closest to him. In many people's minds, Tony would be considered a waste, a throwaway, someone in need of a good old-fashioned butt-whuppin'. But to Cheryl and me, Tony is an angel sent by God to be our son's best friend. Although Tony has brought a lot of pain on his own family, he has been one of the more practical blessings to our family. Tony will come over and take Ryan fishing up in the mountains, buy him lunch, and make sure he always has enough ranch dressing for his French fries (of which Ryan requires boatloads). Yet I know that after he drops Ryan off, Tony drives away wondering how he's going to hold his own life together. Tony is an absolute train wreck, but behind all the brokenness, immaturity, and instability is a side of Tony that is good. It may take a few years to uncover it, but Tony has a pure heart. Sinful, but pure.

Maybe you know someone like this, someone who would not rate very high on the "spiritual scale," someone who has maybe been broken by the sin of others or by their own poor choices, or both—and because of that, they sin a lot. Maybe it's a family member, an acquaintance, a troubled youth, or a waitress who used to be a "dancer," and not of the ballroom variety.

Jesus had many friends like these. Whether it was the corrupt IRS agent Levi, the prostitute who anointed him, or the burly Roman centurion who asked Jesus to "help my unbelief" (Mark 9:24 NKJV), Jesus loved being around these folks. Instead of microjudging their dysfunction, he opposed those who got in the way of them finding his grace. In fact, his calling was to the messed up among us. Jesus said, "It is not the healthy who need a doctor, but the sick. I have not come to call the righteous, but sinners" (Mark 2:17).

Jesus told a story in Luke 14:16–24 about a man who invited many guests to a great banquet. When they declined, the master essentially said, "Forget them, and go to all the outsiders and invite them in!"

Jesus has favorites. They are not always the best behaved, nor the most religious, but they are loved by God. They are the ones who know they need help, and the ones who show up when invited to come over. They are the ones truly grateful for any nice gesture they are granted.

Ten Hurdles of Holiness

Within the Jewish worldview people grew up believing in ten degrees of holiness, each level moving from an outer to an inner circle, becoming closer and closer to God. Those considered most holy, therefore, were the few priests allowed in the inner sanctum. The least holy folks would reside farthest from the place of sacrifice and worship, the Holy of Holies.

Jews believed Israel and the city of Jerusalem were akin to the outermost rings of holiness in God's eyes. The third ring of religious society might be considered the Temple Mount in Jerusalem, where anyone could go. Peasants and paupers hung around a lot because the profits for panhandling were higher when they mingled with others who were, at least for that moment, thinking about God.

Inside the Temple Mount was the fourth ring. It was called the Court of the Gentiles. Within these porticoes around the temple was a large paved yard where the rare proselytes were admitted and where a worshiper could buy their own animal to have the priests and Levites slaughter it. Although Gentiles were allowed here, you would go only if you had really thick skin. For it was in the Court of the Gentiles that a stone lattice wall was erected with one gate, through which only the Jews could pass. (Imagine, if you will, the water fountains of the Jim Crow South where, though black people were allowed to drink water, they were not allowed to drink from the superior "whites only" fountains.) Along this wall were Latin and Greek graffiti prohibiting anyone but a Jew to enter. Death was sure and swift for any non-Jew trespassers. From here on in, only the Jews could get closer to the holy place, but there were still levels of acceptance and clear lines in the religious sands for who was in and who was out.

The next circle, going inward, was called the Court of Women, for obvious reasons: females only. Following that was the Court of the Israelites, where only men and priests could go. Next was an open area surrounding the temple

154

and the altar, and here only the religious pros were allowed: priests and Levites. Edging closer to the middle was the eighth circle, which was a strip of pavement between the altar and the exterior porch of the temple. The ninth inner circle was the sanctuary inside the temple, where you could see the symbols of true holiness: the table of shewbread, the golden candlestick, and the altar of incense. And then, finally, only one man, the high priest, could walk through a heavy linen curtain and enter the Holy of Holies. This small room was completely dark, and once a year it would be graced by the appearance of God.

Imagine what it would feel like if you could or could not go certain places based on your family of origin. Imagine a place where you'd always be judged by rules and centuries-old lines of demarcation. What if, when your children got sick, your church leaders came to you and asked, "What sin have you done that allowed God to punish you like this?" Imagine how you'd feel if you, as a Gentile, came close to the church or temple, and your rambunctious son mistakenly ran into the Court of Women and was immediately cut down with a sword. Imagine the false worship of arrogant people who had climbed the ladder of success and who, although they lived no differently than you, could look down on you from their superior place and dismiss your honest quest to find God. It just doesn't seem right, does it?

Well, it wasn't right, and this is one reason why Jesus spent his days on earth trying to remove religious barriers that kept the pure in heart from coming to him. Then he asked his apprentices (hopefully you and me) to continue this deconstruction.

Jesus on a John Deere

Jesus understands and sees into a heart and mind in a way no human can. When he sees someone, he sees their history, their chemical makeup, the brutal world system around them, the effects of both their own sin and the sin of others around them, and the wiles of demonic forces constantly trying to tear them down.

In college I worked at a prison for adolescent sex offenders. These kids were the very worst of the worst, and the crimes they committed would probably make you immediately call for their eternal punishment. Initially, as I heard what each person had done, I wanted to write them off myself. But week by week, month by month, as I read their personal history reports, I began to soften toward them. Every one of them had been severely abused, abandoned, and sexually traumatized. When I began to talk with them and fight to get behind the broken front doors of their behavior, I found young men who did have a heart. As the summer went on, I could not stand in judgment any longer. I saw more clearly how they were acting out, for the most part, from what they'd been taught. They were caught in an abuse cycle from the pit of hell.

I think of myself as a pretty open-hearted guy, but certain personalities and types of sin are harder for me to forgive than others. However, because of my experience that summer, I've realized only God can judge because only he sees the whole picture. And in that whole picture, there is no perfect human being. All of us sin, fall short, and need grace. Christians often create their own criteria for who is most holy, who deserves to stand just a wee bit taller and closer to God. You may have experienced this subtle—or not so subtle—religious hierarchy, even in churches that have the word *grace* in their names.

Interestingly, in the book of Hebrews, Jesus is referred to as the new High Priest. The Jews and Gentiles of that day knew that the high priest's job was to go into the Holy of Holies once a year and carry out the prescribed ceremonies. But they also knew it really didn't make a lasting difference in real life. The high priest knew he would have to redo the whole thing again next year. The writer of Hebrews speaks of Jesus as our new high priest but makes it very clear that his priesthood was in direct contrast to the priestly system that came before his death. The resurrected Jesus is now the one who not only died for the sins of the people once and for all but also abolished all ten circles, the barriers of division and spiritual judgment. No more "in or out." Everyone has a smooth pathway to God.

Because of Jesus's payment, once and for all, God would not create or allow *any* barrier between himself and the people he loves, his favorites, the pure in heart.

And who are the pure in heart? Those people who, though they may be broken and naive, spiritually unsophisticated and less privileged, are truly looking for God.

If I were a filmmaker I would create a scene where Jesus drives a huge bulldozer up the hill toward the temple and rips down every wall while beeping his huge horn at all the priests and Levites, who would be angrily waving their hands at him. Ignoring them, he'd keep on cutting a huge pathway all the way up to the front door of the holy place. All the peasants would be squinting to look through the plume of dust and rubble as they witnessed Jesus put the dozer into second gear, ram up the huge stairs, and blast through the massive wooden doors. And as the high priest ran for his life, Jesus would haul it into the place the people had only dreamed of seeing—the presence of God.

Although the religious barriers would have been removed, the pure in heart, in my imaginary scene, would be standing motionless—mouths open, eyes as big as Frisbees, wondering what this now means for them. Then Jesus, the new King and High Priest, would climb off the John Deere, take his goggles off, run back down the hill, and grab little kids by the hands. He'd put his arm around the prostitutes; he'd pick the beggars up off the ground and summon every person he could find.

Then Jesus would wink and say, "Come on, you who have been trying to find the real God. Follow me." Like the Pied Piper, he'd lead the motley crowd up the hill toward the Holy of Holies, and on the way in he'd stop at the place where an old Jewish man was about to spend his last dollar to pay for a sacrificial dove or pigeon. Jesus would say, "Hey, put your money back in your pocket and leave the animals be. No need for this silliness anymore."

Picture all those people sheepishly but gratefully walking with Jesus. These people are the pure in heart.

Cut. End of scene.

Who's not the pure in heart? All the people who were ticked that Jesus just destroyed their religious constructs, who liked the status quo, who enjoyed creating and propping up their sanctimonious spiritual walls.

The Ministry of Bulldozing

Indulge me for a quick Scene Two. Jesus is standing by the tractor and says to those gathered around him in the newly opened space of the Holy of Holies, "If you're going to follow me, your job is to make sure that the pure in heart can get to me as easily as possible. Because I kicked down the barriers for you, I want you to kick down any barriers you find that keep people at arm's length from my love and acceptance." Then he hands them a key—the key to the tractor that bears the label "ministry of reconciliation." Our job is to reconcile or bring together God's children and their Father and to knock down anything that gets in the way of this happening.

That's revolutionary. That's sacrilegious! People of Jesus, peasants of reconciliation, are those who no longer look at a person's gender, age, color, or attire. They don't care about their denominational affiliation, church background, or sinful behavior. The ministry of reconciling requires that we stop looking at the cover of the book and see the painful storied pages of each person's life as a whole, understanding that their behavior is only the symptom of a sin-ravaged world. As we transcend judgment with understanding and trust in

God's ability to know a person's heart, we will be living out our calling as God's people. Jesus was a man of the half-breed, half-baked, harmed, confused, abused, perplexed, and vexed of soul, and he was about to clean house of all those who drew lines of spiritual demarcation and any barrier that held back his favorites (those seeking him) from finding his grace.

Now it is time to have a serious talk about what I believe is one of the most notorious man-made lines in the sand: the Lord's Supper.

The True Table

"Umm, Pastor Hugh?"

"Yes, little Emily."

"Is it okay if I eat the rest of the communion bread?"

"Are you sure you want to? It's all soggy and everyone's nibbled on it."

"Yep, I don't think Jesus would want it to go to waste."

"Well, I can't argue with that. Go ahead."

A few minutes later five-year-old Emily's parents came up to me and referenced the grape juice stains on Emily's shirt. Apparently she thought that while she was eating the holy bread, she might as well chug-a-lug the fruit of the vine. After we laughed about Emily's request for the communion bread, they asked me how to help Emily understand the meaning of communion. They didn't want it to become "snack time," but they also didn't want to make it the legalistic or separatist experience they had come to know in their religious past. The husband, in fact, had never received communion in that particular denomination because he hadn't completed the religious education classes.

This happened just two weeks after a man left our church over his insistence that communion was only for "serious Christians," as he put it. He was offended that I didn't have, in his words, "a higher fence" around the communion table. His belief was that you should protect the table from half-hearted or wannabe Christians. I asked him how he would determine each week who was worthy to let near the table and who I should bodyguard to keep out. Should we have a little precommunion qualifying test or a bouncer who could remove people from the line? He didn't really have an answer. He said he loved our church but couldn't stay unless we held the fence a little higher. I told him we took a more biblical stance on communion. He got mad, I made him madder, and then I encouraged him to find another church. Okay, I was ticked, so maybe I showed him the door. Pastors are people too.

Of all the issues in the church that are in need of adjustment, our present understanding and practice of communion is perhaps the most significant. We must uncover the essence of what Jesus wanted us to experience in the sacrament of communion so we don't hinder the pure in heart from coming to his table.

Because this is potentially the most divisive chapter in this book, let me start by giving you a few snapshots of my journey as it relates to the communion experience. My inaugural communion memories began in my family's Nazarene holiness tradition. Many denominations shared our church's theological stance that Christ wants us to be holy . . . really holy. I'm still not sure why, but I learned in this tradition that bowling, movies, playing cards, alcohol, soda pop, potato chips or other unhealthy foods, poor grades in school, swearing, and having my butt crack showing from the top of my pants all qualified as being unholy.

In my middle school years, I split time between churches. I often went to my buddy Jon's Catholic church. I didn't like communion there. The wafers were huge, and they absorbed moisture, so if you took it dry, it would invariably get jammed between your tonsils and cut off your air supply. But if you dunked it in the wine, it swelled up, and you felt like you were swallowing your friend's sweaty gym sock. The fear of gagging was powerful, but what stressed me out the most was that I knew my friend's family was essentially smuggling me into the communion line every week. They never said it straight out, but I could see that they wanted to make sure I didn't screw up the arm-crossing thingy. We practiced a lot, but I always approached the priest feeling the pressure of Shaquille O'Neal shooting a free throw. I was sure I'd eventually be exposed and excommunicated, or whatever they do to sinful and unworthy eighth graders.

In high school I learned we Protestants have our own vetting process. While attending the funeral of a friend who'd died in a car accident, my buddies and I were rudely pulled out of a line at the community Lutheran church and told that we were not allowed to participate. The reason? Because the pastor didn't know where our hearts were with God. I told the church bouncer I was a Christian, to which he replied sanctimoniously, "I appreciate your tradition, but I don't know what kind of Christian you are unless you come to this church." So the side lesson I learned while grieving for my friend was that there are Lutheran Christians and non-Lutheran Christians, and non-Lutheran Christians shouldn't take communion in a Lutheran church.

Maybe you recognized your story somewhere in mine. If so, you realize the landmine we're talking about. Even when I shared this book with other publishers, the concerns were clear. One even said, "Hugh, this is a critical issue, and I personally agree that if the church and Christians can understand what you're saying, this could change the very posture of the church . . . but as a conservative Christian company, we don't feel we want to take the heat for this discussion quite yet. Good luck!"

The email from this editor is exactly why I feel the Eucharist is worth fighting over. The worst things about religion are those practices that we intuitively sense are off base but are not courageous enough to defend because of potential opposition. Followers just go with the flow, and crowds prefer not to rock the ship, but a true apprentice of Jesus must be willing to take heat where Jesus did and fight for the things that he would lace up the gloves for. To me, personally, this is a hill worth dying for. Or it's at least worth the risk of receiving a boatload of angry emails. If I succeed in simply opening the door to questioning a tradition that may be just that, a tradition, and not the original intention of Jesus, it will be worth it.

The Pub and the Pulpit

When I lived in Portland, I used to venture downtown to an Irish pub on St. Patty's Day to give the local Celtic wannabes a brief historical sketch of the real St. Patrick. They'd put me on a small stage in the middle of a few hundred beer-swilling Portlanders, and I'd attempt to cut through their green beer–induced fog with the mission of this ancient Christ follower. At the end of each session, I'd ask everyone to raise a glass and toast the three loves of St. Patrick. I'd say, "To his love of the earth," and they'd all yell "Yo!" "To his love of pagan people"—now louder, "Yo!" "And to his love of the real Jesus"—no kidding, they'd get even louder, "Yaaaa!"

I found it interesting that the line to talk to "the Rev" was longer after my pub talk than at any church where I've spoken. Who'd have guessed that the pub could be a fabulous pulpit? Many times, through slurred speech, the partiers would share life's pain or ask honest questions. One guy I fondly remember came up crying and said, "F—ing beautiful, man. F—ing beautiful. I grew up in church my whole life—in fact my dad was a minister—but I've never heard someone talk about God like this. Thank you."

I'm not saying these people are all undercover saints, but over the years I've sure learned that the pure in heart aren't always inside our churches. In fact, many are in places you'd least expect them to be. And many I've talked to used to be in churches until some sort of judgment turned them away. I wonder if Jesus would set a table for these people? In the Appendix I've provided a brief history of how communion came to be. It actually began as a real supper, a love feast of sorts, held on the eve of Passover. Over time, because of the abuses of the "feasting" aspect of celebrating Passover and later Christ's death and resurrection, the pendulum swung the other way. To control who could partake of the wine and the bread, the powers that be began putting walls and restrictions around the sacrament. But in my opinion, from a study of both the history of the church and the biblical texts, I think we swung the pendulum too far and have used communion as a tool to keep people out rather than inviting them in to the mystery of grace.

In 1 Corinthians 11:17–29, we read about how believers were coming together and actually turning the love feast into a free-for-all. Elbowing each other to get the best grub at the table. Getting drunk. Turning a celebration with meaning into a circus. At one point in Paul's admonishment to stop the craziness, he says,

Whenever you eat this bread and drink this cup, you proclaim the Lord's death until he comes. So then, whoever eats the bread or drinks the cup of the Lord in any unworthy manner will be guilty of sinning against the body and blood of the Lord. Everyone ought to examine themselves before they eat of the bread and drink from the cup. For those who eat and drink without discerning the body of Christ eat and drink judgment on themselves. (vv. 26–29)

Often the last part of this Scripture about "examining ourselves" is used to make communion a place where we pause to do a sin inventory. But the context is clear. Paul leveled this rebuke and warning because the early Christians were letting an "agape feast" go wild. It might have felt like watching your aunt Betty get hammered at a church potluck. People were getting drunk, gluttonizing, and toasting to Jesus all at the same time. Watching Christians justify their selfish whims in the name of Jesus, while people in need watched through the window, was most definitely worth a tongue-lashing.

So here's what really ticks Jesus off about communion: he can't stand people who hop up in the communion line every Sunday, receive his grace, and then forget about the needy. And he doesn't want people to unite their "remembrance of him" with acts of selfish indulgence.

Using the "examine yourself" section as justification for us to judge whether someone is or isn't worthy to remember the Lord is just another religious hurdle to get over—or another exercise in missing the point. To truly examine ourselves for "worthiness" should actually cause us to get the heck out of the line until we apologize for our harsh words toward our spouse on the way to church, for failing to give God the best of our finances and time, and for failing to love our enemies, take care of the poor around us, and so on. If someone completely understands the theology around Christ and communion and isn't living her life to the fullness of what she knows, she probably is in a bit more trouble with Jesus than the naive sinner who simply wants to bow before the bread and wine and stumble through the next week trying to figure him out.

On Any Given Sunday

On any given Sunday, in millions of communion lines across the world, there are men who have cheated at work, embittered their children, spent hours surfing porno, or belittled their wives with hurtful words. There are women who bow at the shrine of materialism, exterior beauty, and self-centeredness. There are singles who have not traversed the gauntlet of social parties, dating, and sexual appetites with sinlessness. Our lines of sacrament are full of smokers, gambling addicts, crooked politicians, priestly pedophiles, arrogant pastors, prostitutes, yoga instructors, and, yes, even lawyers! And guess what? That's how Jesus wanted it.

Communion wasn't to be a reward for a certain level of Christian devotion. Jesus gave the bread and wine to men he knew would betray him that very night. He didn't make the disciples sit there with their heads down for twenty minutes examining their lives. He was a man asking his friends to be friends to the world. He knew they would fail him. The Supper would now be a reminder of his grace-filled presence in the midst of their all-too-human struggles. Did Jesus worry about these guys taking his grace for granted? Not really. He was certain they would. He knew they'd have plenty of trials ahead that would test their endurance and devotion as they went out on a mission for him.

Do people take his grace for granted in the church today? Absolutely, and all the time. I probably take God's grace for granted dozens of times in any given day. And if you are honest, so do you. God is big enough to love and welcome us in whatever state we are in.

My point is this: Jesus didn't seem overly concerned about who was at his table. One of the most sacrilegious things Jesus did, which often gets overlooked, is that he served Judas and Peter the wine and the bread. Think about that. Jesus knew both Peter and Judas were going to betray him in the next twenty-four hours, yet he shared bread and wine with both of them. That's revolutionary.

"But," someone might ask, "how do we make sure people don't misuse or minimize the meaning of Christ's sacrifice if we open up communion to 'whosoever will come'?"

The answer: You can't. Nor is that to be a concern. Remember, Christianity is a faith of the heart. Any act of worship, act of service, act of learning, or act of life is always the result of pure faith mixed with impure faith. In truth, no person totally understands Christ. If we're honest, we can remember hundreds of Sunday church services where we were not fully engaged. And how about the thousands of days we've hung on to whatever belief we have by a thin spiritual thread? Even worse are the days we blatantly put our faith on the shelf so we can indulge vice, sin, and selfish living. Yet the table remains an open invitation from Christ to us. To deny people the Supper of our gracious Lord because of behavioral failures, immaturity, or a less than 100 percent understanding of every point in the New Testament is to deny the centrality of grace, and to deny grace is to deny the very foundation of Christ's new kingdom and this faith we call Christianity.

You don't need to worry about protecting God from bad followers. He's a big boy! To be sure, we shouldn't turn a blind eye to our collective hypocrisy or minimize Christ's payment for our continual screwups, but we've got to set a bigger table and realize the wideness in God's mercy. In fact, every time we invite people to share in our remembrance of Christ's broken body and generously flowing blood that covers us all, it is a perpetual invitation to "come as we are" and meet Jesus for the first time or fall a little deeper in love with him.

Here's a deep theological truth that we in the evangelical church need to sticky tab to our dashboards: God is not an idiot! He can't be faked out. You won't get to heaven and find people hiding in dark alleys whispering, "Hey dude, come over here. . . . I just pretended to be a Christian so I could do business networking, but I made it in . . . hee hee!" So why not leave the judging of a man's heart up to the only One who can see that deep and judge correctly? At least in this way, the pure in heart can join us.

Finding Jesus at the Table

In our main Adullam gathering, we take communion every time we meet. It's central to everything we do. We take it at leadership gatherings, and sometimes we take it in our smaller community times. In almost every case people are with us whom we know nothing about, spiritually speaking, except that they came to our gathering that day. This alone signifies to us that they are seeking God at some level. Invariably I say something like this:

> We're now going to remember Christ and take communion together. The bread represents his body. Although Jesus was God, he came for thirty-three years in a human suit and tasted the world like you and I do. He knows how hard it is to be good, to be perfect, but he was, and therefore he let his body get broken for you. The wine or juice in this cup represents the blood Jesus shed on the cross, and as we drink it we remember that God's forgiveness flows freely over anyone who's done anything bad, anytime, even over and over again. Communion is not for you if you had a great week and didn't sin. It's for you who have sinned. It's not for you if you know everything about Christ and have your theology all figured out. It's for anyone who wants to know Jesus better and find out more about him. It's not for you if you have all your ducks in a row. It's for you who have no ducks under control. So if you'd like to remember Christ's body broken for you and blood shed for you, please come.

I can't begin to tell you all the beautiful stories that come from our communion times. Every week around the table is the most visible evidence of God's work in people's lives. Just this last Sunday, as I watched our people line up, I noticed a girl who had been coming for four weeks. For those four weeks she sat watching others receive communion without participating. She would nervously rock back and forth, holding her son on her lap. She was a "dancer" of the worst kind. Probably a prostitute. She had grown up in church enough to know what the Eucharist meant and was honest enough not to participate. But on this day I saw her, with tears in her eyes, stand up, take a deep breath, grab her son's hand, and enter the line.

Behind this young mother and child was a young Jewish girl who's been meeting with me for almost a year, trying to process Jesus as the Messiah. She watched her husband, a Christian, stand up without her and go to the table week after week. Often I saw her tear up, and over coffee together she once shared how sad she is that she isn't ready to share this deep expression of faith with her new husband. She told me how she so much wants to believe in Jesus but just isn't there yet, and she beautifully expressed how she doesn't want to take communion until it reflects the true change in her heart. I told her how much I appreciated her honest processing but let her know that she can still stand in line with her husband to support his faith in Christ. Sure enough, the next Sunday, I tearfully watched her hold his hand and stand by him as he took the body and blood of Christ. My prayer for this woman is the same prayer I know others have prayed over me and that I have prayed over my own children: that God will continue to reveal himself in his own timing. I know someday she'll not only support her husband's faith journey but participate with him.

Watching her and many others over the years has confirmed that when you open up the table, people take it more seriously, but when you allow a subjective curtain of judgment to remain, you actually reduce its impact.

My favorite story of communion is actually from Luke 24. Two sojourners were bummed out as they walked along a road to Emmaus. They had been following Jesus with curiosity all the way to the cross, but then their hero, Christ, was killed. So they walked together silently, wondering what to do with their faith that now seemed worthless.

Notice what Jesus did with these two depressed dudes. After sneaking up behind them and walking with them for a while, giving them glimpses of hope, he then stayed at their home. Luke 24:30–31 says, "When he was at the table with them, he took bread, gave thanks, broke it and began to give it to them. Then their eyes were opened and they recognized him." What a cool story. Breaking the bread with Jesus pulled them out of their disillusionment. Don't miss this: *they recognized Jesus when he broke bread.* The reason I invite the disillusioned, disheartened, and confused to the table is because it is often in the process of "breaking bread" with other believers, in a mystery I don't completely understand, that folks begin to see and long for Jesus.

Jesus is always about the real deal. His concern is always about our hearts. Are our hearts humble, open, and seeking him even while we are doubting, questioning, and ignoring him at the same time? To the nerds and the naive, the know-it-alls and the ne'er-do-wells, Jesus opens his arms and his table and says, "Come." And as we participate in this sacrament, God's grace shows up for one and all.

 To consider: Think about what barriers may be standing in the way of your friends or your own children coming toward Jesus and how you might eliminate them.

 To do: Identify, bless, and become a friend with someone like Tony.

When someone lamented how so many servicemen and poor were given bread only after they sat through a sermon, Oswald Chambers remarked, "They came to eat . . . not hear a sermon."

10

BRINGING HEAVEN TO EARTH

The No-Spin Zone for the Sabbath and Sabbath Giving

Blessed are the peacemakers,
for they will be called children of God.

Matthew 5:9

A handful of people from Adullam have committed significant time to a deeply impoverished group of people in La Chureca, Nicaragua. La Chureca is a city within a trash dump. Adults and children endure thick black smoke from the constant burning of rubber tires, plastics, and other debris as they forage for food and goods to sell for their meager living. They live in squalor. Drugs and violence are pervasive, and many of the young girls face lives of forced prostitution on top of their already brutal existence.

171

These are pictures of Mercedes from La Chureca, Nicaragua. What's amazing is that in many of the pictures we took of her, Mercedes looks thirty years old. Her face is tired, reflecting the toll of her life without peace. Other pictures, however, reveal the thirteen-year-old she was. These more youthful pictures were taken after our friends began to relieve her stress, show her light, and bring some much-needed peace and rest to her soul. In a short time away from trauma and horror, exhaustion, and paralyzing fear, this little girl was able to taste peace. And you can see the difference. (To see more pictures of La Chureca, go to www.lovelightand melody.org.) © Brian Nevins

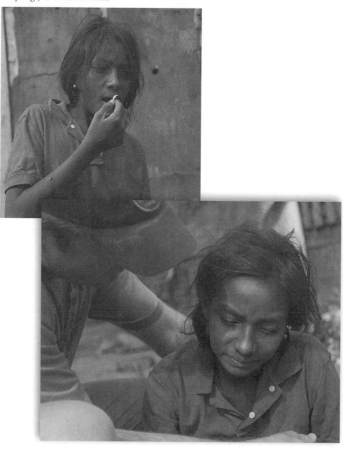

Over the last five years, a girl named Mercedes became the center point of our ministry there. When our team first met her, she was only nine. She was filthy. She was addicted to crack, and her face looked like a thirty-year-old's due to the stress and trauma of being exploited.

As the years went by, a team of kingdom souls would give her respites from her world. They loved her, bathed her, clothed her, sang to her, and taught her to surf, all in hopes she'd be willing to leave the abusive life she was stuck in and stay permanently in a safe home where she could be free.

For most of us reading this, it's hard to identify with someone like Mercedes. But we have all experienced moments of incredible relief. Maybe some of these will help us get a glimpse of how good peace feels, even if it's just for a moment:

- Finding one of your children after you thought he or she was truly lost or could have been abducted
- Receiving an unexpected financial gift in the mail when you were completely broke
- Finally getting those credit cards paid off
- Getting a clean bill of health after a long battle against cancer or another life-threatening illness

The world Jesus dropped into was not a peaceful one. People lived with sickness, constant fear of war, religious persecution, and the daily struggle to stay warm, protect their children, and keep food on the table. Just to have a moment's peace would have felt like heaven!

A Slice of Heaven Here and Now

Do you ever think about heaven? You know, what it will really be like? As a kid (or an adventurous adult), did you ever climb a tall tree to escape the dark, closed-in forest and see everything from a loftier perspective? I think the hope of heaven serves a similar purpose. It helps bring perspective when we consider another life, veiled but just on the other side of our temporal existence. The "kingdom of God" Jesus spoke of has both an earthly and a heavenly meaning. The whole purpose of living a "kingdom life" here is to bring moments, glimpses, impressions of heaven to earth. So it's helpful to visualize heaven both for the joy it will bring in the afterlife and to catch what's happening there so we can bring some of it to our everyday world, here and now.

I remember occasions when I was growing up when my Grandma Mo cozied up next to me on the flower-print sofa to watch Lawrence Welk. It was bad enough to have to smell the mentholated Vicks VapoRub that she would smear just below her nose to alleviate her snoring disorder. But being stuck watching Lawrence Welk, for an active eight-year-old kid, was brutal! I remember that one time Grandma Mo grabbed my hand and peacefully said, "Hughtommy, this is what heaven's going to be like." At that moment I surmised that heaven would probably smell like a mixture of old people and eucalyptus ointment and sound like an eternity of commercial-free polka. Needless to say, I was not sold on the concept.

In fact, this event scarred me. Most of my life I didn't find much solace in the idea of going to heaven. In my early twenties I remember asking God in prayer not to come back too soon. I requested that he at least wait until I could travel a bit, learn how to surf, and experience the joy of fatherhood. Looking back, all three were a tad overrated, but at the time they seemed a far cry better than floating around in white, cloudy nebulousness, singing hymns all day. Yes, I thought it would be cool to see God, shake Jesus's hand, and grab a latte with Big Mo (Moses, that is, not Grandma Mo), but I figured after that I'd just schlep off to my corner of eternity and watch the clock tick.

If my idea of heaven from back then is anywhere near the zip code of yours, perhaps you can identify with my youthful desire to stay here on earth for as long as possible and put off what I believed would be a boring, mind-numbing eternity to come. If heaven is an afterthought, it makes perfect sense to guard your life, protect your stuff, and generally make sure you live large. Sure, you will help others occasionally, feel bad when you hear stories like those of the poor in La Chureca, recycle, give a little of your time and money, and maybe pick up a cause or two to support along the way.

But that's about all you will do. In fact, it seems silly to try to engage the deep needs of the world, and true peace activists should be pitied. After all, what's the point? You live, you die, it's over . . . might as well eat, drink, and be merry.

But the real story of heaven is an idea so big, we can't tackle it all now, yet I find it interesting that in his Sermon on the Mount, Jesus continually references qualities we'd find in heaven. Qualities like comfort, mercy, seeing God himself. Then later, in a poignant moment with his apprentices, he teaches them the art of peacemaking through prayer, saying to pray, "Your kingdom come, your will be done, on earth as it is in heaven" (Matt. 6:10). In other words, Christ followers are to hope for, ask for, and involve themselves in activities that bring a little heavenly peace to peaceless earth.

Biblical writers describe wonderful aspects of heaven: no more crying, no more pain, no more suffering. But the quality that most draws my heart is the knowledge that to be in heaven is to experience perfect peace. Ahhhh . . . now that's something I could really get excited about. Jesus says those who bring moments of peace to troubled souls—peacemakers—will be called "the children of God" (Matt. 5:9). But what is peace?

In part, it is the absence of fear, concern, or worry. It's an inner life disposition that is full of meaning, trust, faith, and a sense of intimate connectedness to the Creator of the universe. Peace is not the life of a hippie stoned on weed, living somewhere between reality and Hookah Land to avoid being fully present and alive to life. It is not shirking off true responsibilities. It's not about avoiding work and commitments. It's about complete shalom.

On my trip to the Middle East, while walking the dark streets of occupied Bethlehem, one of our leaders told me the real meaning of shalom. It is peace in the sense of being in harmony with God, in harmony with community, in harmony with oneself, and in harmony with creation. It's total harmony.

I've met a lot of people who don't buy my particular take on Jesus. But I don't know anybody who doesn't want this type of peace.

Fighting for Peace

Imagine, if you will, the following scene, which actually happened: I pulled into the underground parking lot at Denver International Airport. I parked my Jeep Wrangler, which had its top off, and just as I was turning off the engine, I heard a loud scream from a female. Blowing it off as a possible fluke, I opened my door and walked around to pull my luggage from the backseat. Again I heard a scream, followed quickly by another. *Okay, this is not a happy woman.*

I moved immediately into "save the damsel in distress" mode. Dropping my bags, I quickly reached into my Jeep console and removed my hunting knife. So far, I'd only ever had to use the thing to pick a piece of meat out of my teeth. Oh, and one time I used it to cut the plastic tag off a newly purchased Banana Republic shirt. But other than that, its life as a knife had been pretty tame. But now, feeling my inner Crocodile Dundee awakening, I opened the large blade for serious action. Sprinting toward the source of the screams, which seemed to be about fifty yards away, I was full of adrenaline. *I can't believe I may actually get to use this thing to save someone's life!*

A few feet into my gallop, I became painfully aware of a recently torn hamstring (I did it a week before while running down the first base line during a softball game, doing my best to help out Adullam's team, The Inglorious Batters). But this was a case of life or death! I had to keep moving! I ended up moving one leg really fast while the other one just sort of dragged behind, like Verbal Kint from *The Usual Suspects*. As I rounded the corner, I tightened my grip on the knife and raised the blade in what I hoped was a samurai-worthy stance, just high enough to be ready for physical confrontation.

And that was when I saw the source of the crisis: two high school girls goofing around. Their smiles and girly shrieks turned to stark terror at the sight of me, a forty-three-year-old bald guy poised with a knife, creating a horror movie–sized shadow on the concrete floor.

They screamed.

"Aaaaaaggghhh!" I yelled back. "I'm not going to hurt you! I was coming to save you!"

Then, catching my breath, I asked loudly, "Why are you girls screaming bloody murder in the middle of a dark parking garage anyway? Haven't you seen what happens in parking garages on TV?"

Panting and leaning on the car beside me to steady myself, I gasped, "Please . . . don't . . . do that!"

They quickly apologized, and we all took a few more deep calming breaths together. Then I dragged myself and my throbbing leg back to my Jeep, knife dangling from my visibly shaking hand, thankful my bags were still where I left them.

After pulling myself together on the elevator on the way up to the ticketing counter, I thought, *Nice, Halter. You didn't actually get to save anyone's life and instead managed to scare the crap out of everyone, including yourself.* And then I thought, *Ah well, at least you've got a great story here for your "peacemaker" chapter.*

So let's look at what it really means to be a peacemaker.

Jesus, Prince of Peace

Unlike me, Jesus, who was dubbed the Prince of Peace, was actually required to fight for peace. His birth was announced with a sky full of angels shouting "Peace on Earth!" but his life would end violently on the cross to secure that prophesied peace.

Peace, real peace, doesn't seem to just show up without a struggle. Have you noticed that? Throughout history, thousands of events have demonstrated that peace comes only when it is fought for.

Look again at the last picture of Mercedes smiling. If you just saw that one picture you'd think, "Ah, so peaceful." But what you don't see is the tooth-and-nail battle that took place to save her life. She experienced a peaceful oasis only because God's people put thousands of dollars on their Visa cards and booked six-hour flights from Denver to go be with her six to eight times over several years. Once on the ground, these folks would pray to find her, pray when they found her, and give their time completely to helping her out of a peaceless existence. Eventually, tragically, Mercedes died of complications caused by AIDS. But because of a handful of people who loved her, she knew some moments of earthly peace, was introduced to the Prince of Peace, and now lives in total, complete peace in heaven.

This is the call of Jesus: to be a peacemaker.

Pure Religion

Do you ever wonder what real effect Christians as a whole have in terms of bringing peace to our world? How much actual good goes out to our planet through the combined financial gifts and tithes we pump into church coffers each Sunday? It may surprise you to hear that the average church in America spends about 85 percent of its income on itself— money to support the church programs, staff, and facilities.

Much good comes from these things, no doubt, but at a conservative estimate, we have about 400,000 churches in America, and they average about 70 people per church, with a median annual budget of about $100,000. I'll let you do the math, but suffice it to say, if we leaned up a bit on the new carpet, stained glass windows, and "family centers" and made sure 50 percent of our collected resources went to the more desperate needs of people outside our church walls, our faith probably would be the most respected in the universe!

So what's the point? Any honest look at what our religion actually produces in terms of blessing, helping, or bringing peace to the world we live in reveals a sad reality: not nearly enough. Yes, we have some Christians giving their money and time to others in true need in astounding ways. And those people are a bright hope. But the percentages don't lie. In truth, there's little balance in what the church gives to itself versus what we give to those who have next to nothing.

The book of James defines simply and clearly what God considers to be "pure and faultless" religion—or in other words, what God considers the "real deal" in kingdom language. It is simply "to look after orphans and widows" (1:27). Out of all we do (including "spiritual disciplines") and all we spend our money on in the name of God, what appears to please God the most is caring for those in dire need and thus bringing a little heavenly peace to the world.

Sacrilege and the Sabbath

This Sunday we're not having a church service at Adullam. Instead, our entire church is going to serve the poorest neighborhood in Denver by teaching the kids to play lacrosse, having a huge barbeque, and facilitating an art and music fair, followed by an outdoor concert. We're learning as a community how to make the Sabbath make sense again. Please don't think this is a wild act. It's just a baby step closer to what I think Jesus might have us do on Sunday.

We've talked about bringing peace and making peace, and now we've got to talk about our weekly rhythm of going to church and how we can get back to God's design for Sabbath. I know what you're thinking: "Hugh, the Sabbath is a day of rest, and God said that the Sabbath was made for man. So please tell me you're not going to mess with this tradition too, are you?"

You've read this far in the book, so you probably know by now that yes, I'm about to stir things up again. There are simply too many biblical stories that challenge our basic understanding of "church day."

I've already mentioned several stories where Jesus used the Sabbath day to help people. I can't help but wonder if he actually deliberately waited until the Sabbath to do his best healings and helpings. He almost seemed to be trying to make a point. Maybe we should take this to heart.

Throughout the Gospel records are many stories of how the Pharisees were either following Jesus, hoping they'd catch him screwing up, or hanging out and being appalled at what he was doing on the Sabbath. They got their loincloths in a bunch because he healed and helped out with the practical concerns of others instead of attending the synagogue. They found it completely absurd that his boys would pick wheat and eat it as they walked through the fields, and they really got cranky when they heard that Jesus would spend both Friday and Saturday nights out on the town eating with lowlifes like Levi and other non-Sabbatarian outcasts.

Have you ever imagined the rumors that flowed through Nottingham about Robin Hood and his habit of stealing from the rich and giving to the poor? That's how I imagine a groundswell of whispers moving through the streets and the countryside of curious Jews and Gentiles. Although the accounts people heard of Jesus's "troublemaking" might have originally made them bristle, I can easily imagine a father and mother glancing at each other across the dinner table and sheepishly smiling as if to say, "Yeah, but there's something I love about this guy."

The peasants loved Jesus for the same reason the African American community listened intently through their static radios to Joe Louis fighting Max Schmeling back in 1938: he fought for the underdog. They wanted Jesus to win out over the religious leaders, because when he did, it made the world, or at least that day, better. They knew at a gut level that his way of living made more logical sense. Even if they didn't put their faith fully in him, behind closed doors they must have said, "Look, I don't know if this man is really the Messiah, but man, oh man, would I love for God to be like him. He actually helps people; he doesn't let the religious traditions get in the way of lending a hand or having a party. I could love a God like that."

Because our culture no longer sanctions any "sacred days," weekends can be the busiest times of the week. Minivans full of kids head for soccer games, schools host art and sporting events, and a third of all the people in the United States now work on Saturday and Sunday. So what are we supposed to do? Jam the already jacked-up Sunday with more "to-dos"?

I wonder if we could learn from Jesus and think outside the box. Maybe we could shoot for a little peace for ourselves and a little peace for someone else.

In our church we ask our people not to come every week. Most of our people are connected to incarnational communities where they band together and try to learn the life of Jesus together. So it makes perfect sense to encourage them to take some Sabbath days and lend a hand to each other or take a walk through a wheat field or a burning dump. Not only is this freedom appreciated, but people tell me how meaningful it is to get the kids in the minivan to head to the park or the inner-city projects instead of to the church now and again.

Because of Jesus, the Sabbath is open for new business!

How Jesus Would Start a Church

Some friends of mine, Brandon and Jen Hatmaker, are pastors of Austin New Church. I joke with Brandon about the name since the church is already three years old, but the story of their beginnings gives us a glimpse into what Jesus might see as a wonderful use of our Sundays. Their story is chronicled in the book *Barefoot Church*, and in it Brandon shares how one day he felt God saying to him, "Brandon, you don't love the poor." It hit him hard enough that he left his well-salaried position as a staff member of a large church to serve the poorest in urban Austin. He didn't begin with the intention of starting another church; he just wanted to let God teach him how to serve "the least of these" (Matt. 25:40).

What happened fairly quickly is that a bunch of ex-churchgoers, those who had grown tired of just going to church and playing the game of self-focused religion, heard about the opportunity to serve and joined in. It was surprisingly appealing to a bunch of non-churchgoers as well. Community formed, and before long, that community turned Brandon's original mission to the poor into an actual church.

Here's a cool question: What if you'd never grown up in church and had no memory of institutional faith, and instead of God giving us an entire Bible, he gave us only the four Gospels, Acts, and the one verse in James that defines pure religion as looking after widows and orphans? If everyone just said, "Okay, let's do that!" and set off to find every orphan and widow in need, what might our churches look like? How might they form? How would they be perceived?

You now have a picture of a sacrilegious church that might actually change the world.

The book of Acts says that in the early communities, "There were no needy persons among them" (4:34).

Incredible! The peasants within earshot surely must have said, "Now these people are my type of folk. If there is a church like this that uses their time and money to help the needy instead of lining their pockets, I might consider joining it."

A Sacrilegious Sunday

In his letter to the Colossians, Paul wrote to new converts hoping to keep them from getting sucked into religious formalities instead of looking for true needs they could help meet. "Therefore," he wrote, "do not let anyone judge you by what you eat or drink, or with regard to a religious festival, a New Moon celebration or a Sabbath day" (Col. 2:16). In other words, he warned them not to get caught up in ceremonial religion—not even Sabbath keeping.

Yes, our Scriptures encourage and challenge Christ followers to Sabbath, and we also have a warning in Hebrews for those who make a habit of "non-gathering." But you'll notice from this passage in Hebrews 10:25 that even their gatherings were about others and meeting the needs of others: "And let us consider how we may spur one another on toward love and good deeds, not giving up meeting together, as some are in the habit of doing, but encouraging one another—and all the more as you see the Day approaching." For early faith communities, their "church" experience was much more raw, and meeting needs of those in and out of the community was as much of their focus as we might put on a sermon or worship.

What do we learn? That you can't really be a Christ follower without having consistent rest and refocus, but also that our spiritual gatherings have some flexibility and opportunities that go way beyond our "just going to church" mentality. Our religious rhythms must be good news to the neighborhoods, communities, and cities we worship in.

Sacrilege and Tithing

It may sound strange to bring up the idea of tithing in a book like this, but when you consider how often the world links money with our present idea of a Sunday church experience, I believe it's an elephant in the room that should be addressed. If you ask people who aren't involved in a church why we Christians put so much emphasis on going to church, most think it's because we need the dough. And if you ask some of the 25 million Christians who have left the church why they split, you'll find that many of them got tired of putting so much time and money into buildings and programs and a staff of dozens—rather than into places and people who were impoverished, hurting, and in the deepest sort of misery and need.

Closely associated with our consumeristic church experience is a concept called the tithe. To tithe means to give a tenth of your income to God, and it has been a discipline and expectation of Christian life for a long time. Even though the average Christian gives only 2 to 3 percent of their income to the church (which, by the way, is about the same percentage that non-Christians give to charity), most God-fearing saints who grew up in church know that for some reason they're supposed to give 10 percent of their income to the church.

Out of loyalty, love of Jesus, or blind acceptance, many folks have lived by this rule. Actually, for the most part, I find most are quite happy they are givers. Many suggest that by setting aside 10 percent of their income for others, they feel an overall sense of living a blessed life. Some are proud that their consistent giving has helped support the church and its ministries. They appreciate the work of the pastors they support and find giving a natural part of being faithful to God. Yet others feel ripped off. They add up the dollars they've put into the institution and lament the lack of "return" on their investment. They are skeptical that the money they give is really being used to make a significant and positive difference in the real world. This was my reason for entirely pulling out of church as I once knew it. I wanted to go help a real person with my money. Sadly, I think the issue of tithing would be much more inspiring if we knew where the idea came from.

Meet Melchizedek

Melchizedek (yeah, say that name three times real fast) was the first priest ever. Simply put, he was Abraham's pastor. God told Abe he was going to bless the entire world through his family lineage. Since nothing that good comes easily, he had to fight four cantankerous rival kings in the process. He did eventually win and came out of the woods exhausted but deeply grateful for God's provision and protection. And then the first thing he did was meet up with Melchizedek and give him a "tithe" of the spoils of war.

And thus, from here on out, God's people—from King David to Nehemiah to Solomon and on through all the prophets—felt as though the tithe was the general plan for not only thanking God but also providing for the entire nation. And it worked pretty well. It covered not only the religious affairs but also the welfare kitty. The tithe covered almost every need of the nation. Later, when the Romans occupied the Israelites' homeland, during the time of Christ, people struggled because by then tithing had evolved into another religious law. Added to the tithe were taxes to the Romans and tithes to the temple, and the impoverished were no longer being helped or provided for as they once were.

We need to start here. This is why many Christians don't even bother with teaching about the tithe any more—because it's been so corrupted over time. Now that I've studied biblical history, I realize that the tithe was never even part of the Ten Commandments. It was never meant to be a law.

It was a principle, and in actuality it was a pretty good idea to set aside part of our income to help others. In the Old Testament, and even in Acts when the people brought together or "centralized" their giving, monies were quickly dispersed to bring some tangible help and peace to people in need. So I'm all for collecting funds and bringing it into the storehouse, but let's not forget the back end of that: it was mostly given away to others in deep need. How much fun would that be?

In the New Testament we see "Extreme Tithing"; it comes from the natural desire to love and help one another. People sold houses and land and gave generously, even when in extreme poverty, to the point that "there were no needy persons among them" (Acts 4:34). Wouldn't you love to be part of a church that had no needs? Even better, wouldn't you love to be part of a community that was such a blessing to your surrounding area that no one had any physical needs?

A New Old Way of Tithing

So here's the sacrilegious part of this. If you want to keep more money in your pocket, I'd suggest you become an Old Testament giver, because that will only cost you 10 percent. If you truly want to be a New Testament giver, you have to relate with Jesus and let him have control over 100 percent of your stuff. Now that's sacrilegious. No more mindless giving to the church, but also no more selfish individualism.

Please don't take my whims as your ways, but here's how we approach the matter in our church community. Because the issue of giving is now a matter of the heart instead of law, we encourage everyone toward the tithe as a basic framework for apprenticing your life after Jesus. Ten percent is still a great amount that will help you avoid debt and allow you to experience the blessing of helping others. Yet we think there's a great balance to be struck between centralizing it and decentralizing it. So we encourage people to start by giving 5 percent spontaneously to needs that come up along the natural course of life, and we also encourage everyone to throw in 5 percent toward what we do together, because many of these things will require larger amounts of resources and because we know that we can do more together than by simply living as individuals. So far the spirit of giving in this way is helping people learn to take ownership, live simply, and cheerfully help friends in need, and it keeps us all feeling that we're part of something bigger.

For you pastors who fear only getting 5 percent, remember, you really only get 2 to 3 percent on average, so allowing people to find a balance may actually help you *and* release your people and their resources into the lives of people in the streets.

Sacrilege and Time

Many churches are now taking pure religion and the call to be peacemakers more seriously and not only redistributing funding but also allotting church time to help people serve the world, rather than serve on one more church-focused committee.

On those months which have a fifth Sunday, Austin New Church leaves the building together and goes out to serve the city. Their community groups do the same twice a month, alternating weeks to do what they call "love your neighbor, serve your city." We at Adullam took our cue from this philosophy and also suggest that our villages (as we call our communities) take at least one Sunday off every month or so to help someone in the neighborhood around them. Two years ago, we tried an experiment where we adjusted our church service schedule so that one week we'd gather together and the next week we'd shut the church doors and meet in our communities throughout Denver. One such community that had only five people in it used the time to create a food and clothing co-op that serves fifty low-income families.

As we encourage those in Adullam to follow their hearts and give where God tells them to give, we notice that peace begins to descend, along with renewed freedom and anticipation of where they might spend their money to help someone in need in a tangible way. Religion and church start to make sense.

Yes, hard decisions must be made to accommodate the type of giving that supports peacemaking as a mission. None of our staff members receive a full-time salary. As we let people give to real needs, we don't bring as much into our church kitty. We can't ever consider buying a building or paying for programs. We simply don't have the money to do it. But what we do have is a vibrant community of people who throw in together to *be* the church to each other and the world, instead of simply going to church. It makes sense to us and seems to make sense to those outside the church too.

Peacemaking Sabbaths

Returning to the original story about our church taking a Sunday off to serve the poorest village in Denver, I noticed something powerful happening during that event. My teenage daughters, who historically don't really like church services, joined us downtown. As soon as they stepped foot on the grounds of the community center, they clicked into a beautiful posture of service to the poorest kids and their single moms. Toward the end of the day, I was having trouble finding the girls. I got a little nervous that they had wandered off into some trouble, so I went out on the main street, looked down the sidewalk, and saw them both walking down the street, each carrying a young child on their shoulders, with one of the single moms beside them. They were making sure the little kids got home safe. As they put the children down, the mother hugged both my daughters. On their return, they both asked, "Hey, Dad, why don't we just do this every Sunday?" Great question.

As you consider following Jesus, take account of what you do with your weekends, your Sabbath time, your money, and your friends. Does anything you do culminate in bringing peace to others? I think church can make all the difference in the world. Collectively we should worship. Collectively we should be together. Collectively we can experience deep fellowship and learn the truth of Scripture together. But we don't always have to do all of these things inside a building on Sunday. Peacemaking isn't a static state of mind. It's about being the love of God with work gloves on. It's thoughtfully setting aside some of your money and your time, even your Sabbath, to bring peace to a hurting neighbor, whether they live across the street or on the other side of the world.

 To consider: Where is peace lacking in your immediate world—in your home, in your workplace, in the lives of your friends, or in your neighborhood? Where would Jesus have you begin in bringing peace to these places and people?

 To do: This month tithe your income (give 10 percent) to an actual person you know needs a lift.

 To do: Commit to giving one day a month to fighting one global issue of brokenness such as poverty, the sex trade, or disaster relief.

"All works of love are works of peace."

Mother Teresa

OF XBOXES AND BURNING BUSHES

Rediscovering the Church Jesus Wants to Build

Blessed are those who are persecuted because of righteousness, for theirs is the kingdom of heaven. Blessed are you when people insult you, persecute you and falsely say all kinds of evil against you because of me. Rejoice and be glad, because great is your reward in heaven, for in the same way they persecuted the prophets who were before you.

Matthew 5:10–12

The other day I was leaving a local Starbucks on the way to pick up my daughter from school. This particular Starbucks is known for having one of the most dangerous parking situations imaginable. It's like trying to get in and out of pit row at a standard NASCAR race—you have to be on your game and watch for cars coming from four different directions.

As I slowly backed my car out, looking in my rearview mirror, then quickly to both sides, I apparently failed to see the small, red Porsche convertible that materialized out of thin air. I heard a long, loud, squeaky honk and then, surprisingly, a feminine voice yelling, "Move your a—, idiot!"

Growing up in the hood rendered me generally numb to such tirades, and most of the time I laugh it off. So I slammed my brakes, grabbed my coffee that had spilled during the situation, licked off the lid, and peered over the dash. That's when I saw on the back of her car the ol' Christian fish symbol and a bumper sticker that said, "Honk if you love Jesus."

So I did . . . and I followed her down the back street and held the horn down for about thirty seconds. She then pointed to heaven using her middle digit, so I pulled up next to her, rolled down my window, and calmly bellowed, "I'm just doing what your bumper sticker says, you Christian wacko!"

Not too reverendly, I know, but . . . man, I felt better and relished the experience of being persecuted by yet another Christian.

I wonder if Jesus got persecuted by other religious people. Let's find out:

> Blessed are those who are persecuted because of righteousness, for theirs is the kingdom of heaven. Blessed are you when people insult you, persecute you and falsely say all kinds of evil against you because of me. Rejoice and be glad, because great is your reward in heaven, for in the same way they persecuted the prophets who were before you. (Matt. 5:10–12)

At first glance most people quickly jump to the same conclusion I did when I first read this passage: we should expect persecution if we are people of faith. In fact, if we're really good Jesus people, we'll constantly be looking over our shoulders for empty beer bottles and rocks being thrown at us by the angry pagans!

A few years back I was in San Diego doing some training at a large megachurch. In a room consisting of mostly college students, one young man raised his hand and asked, "I guess I'm having a hard time understanding your encouragement for Christians to be likable people. Jesus was persecuted a lot. And he said we would be too. I don't think Jesus cares one bit whether people like us. Our job is to tell people they're sinners and scare them away from eternity in hell." Then he quoted the words of Jesus I just referenced above.

I had to hand it to this young gun for his sincere desire to follow whatever the Good Book said, at any cost, even if people didn't like him. But there was one slight problem. He assumed persecution would come *only* from outside the church. History does show us that Christians have faced incredible pain from those outside our faith system. Martyrdom is still happening at record pace, and Christians are dying because of their faith and work for God. I don't want to minimize this type of persecution. It's serious! But that's not what Jesus was talking about in this Beatitude. He was trying to prepare his friends for the reality of getting hammered by those *inside* the religious establishment. Jesus knew the first wave would come from inside the family of faith.

Just for kicks sometime, find all the Scriptures where Jesus was getting hassled. You'll find a few times when the Romans kicked the stuffing out of him, but almost every other confrontation he endured was from those inside his Jewish institutional faith system. Whether it was for talking with women, eating with sinners, helping the poor, healing the sick, speaking truth, challenging the financial and political oppressors, skipping a hand-washing ritual, letting prostitutes pour perfume on him, working on the Sabbath, teaching things that appeared different than the law, calling for a better covenant, forgiving sinners, or just walking down the street minding his own business, Jesus was constantly badgered by the religious elite.

It happened to the prophets, it happened to Jesus, and if you decide to apprentice your life after his, you may take a few stones to the forehead too.

In Acts 7 Stephen was trying to help the churchy folk understand the real Jesus. Strategically standing before the religious hierarchy (called the Sanhedrin), Stephen wisely took great pains to explain everything in lingo they could agree with. He walked them through their own shared history, starting with Abraham, then Moses, and finally he showed them that God no longer inhabits or hangs out in the temple, but he's now a God of the people and lives in the hearts of those who love him.

I can imagine as he began his story, looking at their faces, he might have thought, *Okay, they're tracking with me; they are getting it.* But as he quoted to them their own Scriptures, verses that prophesied God would leave their religious zones of manmade control, Stephen must have seen the veins in the audience members' necks start to expand, their eyebrows start to raise, their jaws start to clench. So he says,

> You stiff-necked people! Your hearts and ears are still uncircumcised. You are just like your ancestors: You always resist the Holy Spirit! Was there ever a prophet your ancestors did not persecute? They even killed those who predicted the coming of the Righteous One. And now you have betrayed and murdered him—you who have received the law that was given through angels but have not obeyed it. (vv. 51–53)

From the days when Moses had to deal with a bunch of griping ingrates in the desert (God's "chosen people") to the time when Zechariah was stoned in the courtyard of the temple by order of King Joash (because the prophet had denounced the people for their unfaithfulness; see 2 Chron. 24) to the time of the apostolic movement of the early church, trouble often came from the religious.

Trippin' over Jesus?

Let's now return to the question asked by the young man from San Diego. If Jesus said we'd be persecuted, and if the biblical writers said that Jesus would be a stumbling block to people, can't we just be jerks for Jesus and accept the consequences as par for the course?

The idea of being a stumbling block is a unique picture. It could be anything that people might trip over: a root sticking out from a tree, a loose stone, or a large impediment keeping someone from getting where they are trying to go. Romans 9 says,

> What does all this mean? Even though the Gentiles were not trying to follow God's standards, they were made right with God. And it was by faith that this took place. But the people of Israel, who tried so hard to get right with God by keeping the law, never succeeded. Why not? Because they were trying to get right with God by keeping the law instead of by trusting in him. They stumbled over the great rock in their path. (vv. 30–32 NLT)

Who stumbled? The Jews, the insiders, the religious. What caused them to stumble? The "great rock" in their path, namely Jesus's message that it ain't about religion anymore, but simple faith. No more law, just grace. Yet so many people believe in Jesus but still approach the world with the law, become hated, and think they are doing God a favor.

Did Jesus cause the heathen to stumble? Well, at worst, it says, they considered the cross "foolishness" (1 Cor. 1:18), but foolishness implies they didn't get it. But the Scriptures are pretty clear that the peasants liked Jesus! Why? He stood up to the powers that were belittling them, and he helped quite a few of them out. He was a man of the people and never held the law over their heads.

Here's the big light bulb every apprentice must see: if you live like Jesus, people will love you! They should also be intimidated by your holiness, perplexed by your faithfulness, and convicted by your righteousness, but for sure you will be loved because you treat them as Jesus would treat them.

Ecclesial Anarchy

I know this will not come as a surprise anymore, but I've been in a lot of trouble with Christians. Here's a list of precious memories. Grab a tall cup of coffee and relax; it will take a while to read. I've been in trouble with Christians for:

- not "tithing" off my paper route income in third grade (this got me spanked with a wooden spoon by my Grandma Mo)
- not coming to my high school youth group more
- coming to my high school youth group, but bringing some shady friends with me
- having CDs of Billy Idol, U2, AC/DC, and Amy Grant— yes, Amy Grant, because she "crossed over" into the "satanic secular" music industry. Yeah, the same industry to which Bing Crosby, Lawrence Welk, and Kenny G sold their souls.
- keeping a brand-new 1990 Isuzu Trooper that was given to me by a friend. In those days, a Honda Accord was the nicest car a pastor should drive to model simplicity and humility.
- not preaching exegetically (line by line, verse by verse)
- not using the King James Version. Apparently God only speaks and understands early seventeenth-century English, preferring liberal uses of thous, wheretofores, and henceforths.
- letting our kids watch Barney and go to Disneyland. Word on the street was that both were of the devil.

- participating in Halloween instead of going to the lame "harvest parties" that other local churches were putting on
- drinking beer, consuming wine, eating red meat, puffing on a cigar (once a year), and buying cereal from Kellogg's (because they were owned by Mormons)
- having a tattoo and letting my kids get tattoos, belly studs, and nose studs
- marrying a woman who had been divorced
- leaving the church league basketball team in order to play for the beer league boys
- challenging my seminary Greek prof's notion that I wasn't worthy of being a pastor unless I spent forty hours a week studying the Scriptures in the original Greek (I got kicked out of class)
- challenging my theology instructor's assertion that wine in Bible times was actually nonalcoholic grape juice (I got kicked out of this class too)
- talking to eighteen-year-old prostitutes, and especially for giving them a hug
- inviting secular musicians to play in our worship band

Seriously, I'm forcing myself to stop here because I could keep going for several more pages until I created a pamphlet called "1,001 Things Hugh Has Done That Have Ticked Off Christians."

Out of all the rocks to the forehead, one that really got me heated was when another pastor called me an "ecclesial anarchist." I decided to confront this accusation head-on, and the lunch appointment was set.

The first thing I asked was, "Since we've never really met, what makes you think that I actually want to tear the church down, especially since I pastor one?" For the next hour he proceeded to drill me with question after question: "What do you think about end times theology? What about women's roles in the church? What about the importance of sermons? What's your view of discipleship? Worship?"

I tried to keep up the pace, feeling more like a contestant on *Jeopardy* ("I'll take Theology for Control Freaks for one hundred, Alex.") than an equal brother in Christ having a give-and-take conversation. Finally I said, "Bill, time out. You've got your undies in a bunch. I feel like you've called me Beelzebub the Church Hater because I don't claim to know everything about everything." He suggested that I might not be a good leader unless I nailed in my doctrine and then asked how I would get people to toe the line. I said, "I suppose I'll just keep trying to get them to Jesus and let Jesus address the line." He wasn't satisfied, but the meeting ended well.

I cannot help but wonder, as these debates go on ad nauseam while widows and orphans and the hurting and the homeless go uncared for and unseen, if Jesus doesn't want to smack his hand to his forehead and say, "Where's the love, guys? The one thing I left you on my short to-do list when I left you to mind the Earth store was 'love one another as I have loved you.' Funny, but I don't remember spending a whole lot of time arguing about how many angels can dance on the head of a pin or showing you how to score well in religious debate. I was too busy healing and helping and encouraging the diseased, the discouraged, and the disoriented. You might consider giving that a shot."

As we come to the end of this book, I hope it has helped you as an individual, but we can't leave it there. Jesus had one more plan. Jesus wants individual apprentices to band together in what he called the church.

The church is actually the problem right now. You know it and I know it. You, your friends, and just about everyone is pretty cool with Jesus. Believe me, he's not the problem. The problem is the overorganized, overreligious, exclusive God-bubbles we call the local church.

And just as we all fight to become true apprentices, we must also fight for the church that Jesus came to birth and lead.

Watch Out for the Leaven of the Pharisees

In an intimate moment with his buddies on a boat, Jesus uses their hunger and desire for bread as an object lesson and says, "Beware of the leaven of the Pharisees" (Matt. 16:6 NKJV). Leaven, of course, was the tiny ingredient that when put into the flour would work its way through and affect the entire loaf of bread, causing it to rise. What was the "yeast" or "baking powder" of the Pharisees? Simply put, it was their iron-clad box of religious laws and traditions that took precedence over simple faith in Jesus. It included written and unwritten expectations that were put upon people like leaden burdens on their souls.

Today, just in America, 25 million Christians do not go to church. These are people who once filled the pews, sang the songs, put money in the offering baskets, and signed the church membership cards. Over the last fifty years they left slowly, like a leak in a hose, drip by drip, but the seam is now bursting open and folks are leaving the buildings and traditions faster than most can imagine. I've spoken to many of these people personally, and when I ask them why they opted out of church, they usually say something like:

"I left to keep my faith."

"I couldn't take it anymore."

"What's the point? Church doesn't really help real people."

"I'd rather be with my real friends on the weekend than sit and sing next to complete strangers."

"I'm tired of giving my money to an institution that just props up its buildings and pastoral salaries."

"I am weary of the silent judgment and archaic expectations to live perfectly."

"I want to make a difference in the real world."

"I don't want to be associated with what the word *Christian* has come to mean in our society."

"I want to live a life of love, not religion or judgment."

What are these folks actually recoiling from? It's not the church as Christ envisioned it; it's the leaven of the Pharisees! Simply put, if Christ's followers would all collectively rip off their stupid bumper stickers and live a life a little more like Christ's, we could not keep the masses away. Although *going* to church is not that big of a deal to Jesus, *being* the church and becoming his winsome representatives does matter to him. A lot.

If you're not sure how confrontational Jesus was to Pharisees in his time, meander over to Matthew 23. In just this one chapter alone Jesus called them "sons of hell," "brood of vipers," "serpents," and "whitewashed tombs" once; "blind guides" and "fools and blind" twice; and "hypocrites" seven times (NKJV). So if you ever thought Jesus was a nice guy, a people-pleaser, or Mr. Loving and wondered if he would stand up to those who make a mockery of religion and church, believe me—he's on your side!

If you've written off "church" because you have picked up on the discrepancy between the way of Jesus and the way of the church, take heart: Jesus has many sacrilegious ideas to help reform the church. Let's bring up a few right now.

Fighting for the Real Holy Ground

A few years ago I was training some pastors in Colorado. At one point in the training, I mentioned how we needed to allow people at all levels of faith and maturity into the life and ministries of the church. I received mostly nodding heads of approval, but one young worship leader came unglued when I shared that we at Adullam let non-churchgoers play in our worship band.

"Excuse me, Hugh, how do you justify letting pagans on the stage?" he asked.

"Well, it's just a stage," I replied.

"Just a stage? It's the most holy place in the church. It's where I lead people into the presence of the almighty God, the place where we prepare for God's Word to be preached. Letting a pagan up there makes a mockery of everything!"

I could tell by his posture and tone of voice that he felt pretty strongly about his convictions. I wasn't looking for a fight, so I simply asked, "Can you find me any biblical support for feeling this way?"

"Of course I can, it's all through Scripture!" he yelled.

"Can you give me some idea of where?"

"Yes! The Old Testament is full of detailed descriptions of how the temple was to be built, and God made it clear that his temple is where he resides, and we'd better honor it!"

A few heads now nodded in agreement with this point, letting me know the audience was pretty confused at this point.

This is the reason we have to be clear about where holy ground is now that the curtain of the temple was literally torn asunder when Jesus breathed his last.

The answer I gave took some time, and I began by deconstructing the pervasive (but extrabiblical) notion that the most sacred spaces continue to be in literal buildings such as temples, churches, or synagogues.

Illuminating Holy Ground

One of the many descriptive names for Jesus is "Light of the World." When light is mentioned, especially in respect to Jesus, it's always juxtaposed against darkness. In the Genesis 1 story of creation, God spoke "light" into a great void of formless darkness. In the New Testament both Paul (in his letter to the Colossians) and the writer of Hebrews mention that Jesus was present at the time of creation, and indeed we could conclude that creation's light foreshadowed the Light of the World's entrance into a dark world a few thousand years later. A study of the word *light* throughout Scripture is, well, illuminating. I highly recommend it. After personally digging into the times and places in Scripture where light broke through and dispelled darkness, I've come to the conclusion that when this happens, sacred space or holy ground appears.

What does that mean for us now? *Sacred space is where light breaks into darkness.*

A friend named Brad helps us see this. Brad was a key member of a band called Dispatch, which gained wide notoriety and a cult-like following for their music but also for their socially conscious focus. They eventually disbanded, but in 2007 they held a reunion concert in Madison Square Garden to raise money for war-torn Zimbabwe.

Brad, now known as Braddigan, has created a nonprofit called "Love Light and Melody," an organization committed to making God's kingdom tangible to the poor and oppressed, mostly through music and loving concern in action. One place they serve is a community of people who live inside a city dump in La Chureca, Nicaragua, mentioned earlier when I shared the story of Mercedes. Along with meeting other physical needs of these impoverished people, once a year Brad holds a "Day of Light" concert in the middle of the dump. He invites musicians, photographers, aid workers, and concerned friends from all over the world to fly in and descend upon this broken community.

This Day of Light perfectly illustrates what a modern-day altar might look like: it is where God's people shed God's love and light in a dark place. You may remember that those from our church who have gone and come back report that La Chureca is one of the darkest, most hellish places they've ever been. Smoke rises constantly from the burning trash. The filth is unbelievable. So the contrast of this special day is incredible. It's a heavenly day when darkness is violently confronted with love and celebration.

Brad and his fellow musicians simply play music all day while others help feed and care for the entire community. This is not your normal Christian concert; in fact, they play mostly secular music that the people are accustomed to hearing on their makeshift radios. The friends Brad invites down to sing and help out with this mission are handpicked, and about half of them aren't following Christ. Yet during this week, and especially this day, "The Day of Light," Christ is the air they breathe, the words they speak, and the impetus for all they offer.

It's sacred space. It is holy ground.

What if holy ground is not in the church building? What if holy ground is those moments when we allow ourselves to be a vessel of light into a crevice of darkness and illuminate the beauty of God's kingdom ways to those groping in a great void? Celtic Christians referred to these moments as "thin places"—places and times when you feel heaven almost touches down to earth because we let God have his way with us and shed some of his light into darkness.

Modern Day Altars of Revelatory Art

Let's keep going on our search for sacred space. After God's light breaks into the world in creation in Genesis 1, we begin to see people making altars to God. It began with Noah creating an altar as an act of gratitude and symbol of a new covenant after the flood. Then we see altars erected in various times and places by Abraham, Moses, Joshua, Samuel, and David, to name a few of the biggies.

In all of these early cases, the altars were built so that sacrifices could be made to God. Most of the time, God didn't ask people to build them. People built them out of a heart response of thankfulness. Until King Solomon's time, all of the altars were built out in nature, under the stars, so to speak. There were no formal tabernacles or temples. In many cases, an altar was simply a few stones put together in a pile large enough to make a fire upon which an animal could be placed.

Although altars became a normal way people worshiped God, we have to remember that God never called them "holy places." They were just important symbols of *human* intentionality toward God. They were most often built as God's nomadic people moved from one place to another, not cemented in a permanent building. Holy ground was found and defined as anywhere people paused to focus on and show gratitude to God.

For a time our church was fortunate to have a worship artist-in-residence named Eric Herron. I asked Eric to join us because with Adullam's desire to worship creatively, outside of the way Americans typically do a church service, I knew we needed someone who could help us rethink the whole worship thing. True confession: I'm not a big fan of singing in public (even tucked away in a congregation), so over the years, you could usually find me outside having coffee during the musical part of worship. Eric taught us the concept of "revelatory art," which essentially means that worship happens anywhere God's people reveal him.

We can all reveal God by supporting both Christian and non-Christian organizations that are serving the least of these. One church in Denver actually organizes benefit fundraisers to help secular organizations. When they do this, the organizations ask, "Why are you doing this for us?" The folks from this church respond, "Because we like to support anyone and any organization that is serving God's interests in the world."

Other ways to reveal God can be to creatively bring attention to one of God's themes like forgiveness, justice, debt relief, or reconciliation, all in order to foster, advocate, or sanction social awareness around you. We know churches that run the live music at a local Starbucks or pub to bring awareness to sex trafficking; others do a benefit lunch at a local school for AIDS relief or local poverty issues. Sometimes it just takes a little creativity to make altars of worship out in the world.

Church of the Nomads

At this point you may be asking, "Yeah, I get your point that holy ground is wherever we pause to bring light to darkness, but didn't God ask Moses to create a tabernacle and give him pretty detailed directions? Wouldn't that suggest that God still wants us to have a sacred place in which to worship? And besides Moses, David also deeply desired to build God a home. Then his son Solomon finally completed the temple of his father's dreams. What of this rich heritage? Doesn't this history suggest that God wants us to have sacred buildings with even holier places within, like, say, the stage and pulpit?"

When David, out of desperate love for God, wanted to build God a place, we find a very, very interesting response from God:

> Go and tell my servant David, "This is what the LORD says: You are not the one to build me a house to dwell in. I have not dwelt in a house from the day I brought Israel up out of Egypt to this day. I have moved from one tent site to another, from one dwelling place to another. Wherever I have moved with all the Israelites, did I ever say to any of their leaders whom I commanded to shepherd my people, 'Why have you not built me a house of cedar?'" Now then, tell my servant David, "This is what the LORD Almighty says: I took you from the pasture, from tending the flock, and appointed you ruler over my people Israel. I have been with you wherever you have gone.'" (1 Chron. 17:4–8)

Even though Solomon got the privilege of building and dedicating the temple, he also understood from his father David's chronicles and conversations with God that the Holy One of Israel transcended that one location. "But will God really dwell on earth with humans? The heavens, even the highest heavens, cannot contain you. How much less this temple I have built!" (2 Chron. 6:18).

Adullam's church gatherings have now met in six different spaces in the six years since we began. We are prone to cancel a service in the building to do a service project, have a day of rest, do a village-only day, or have a picnic or baptism at a local park. So to belong to Adullam you have to be a pretty alert parishioner. Sure, there's a hassle factor to that, but the rewards may surprise you. Apparently God stays on the move with us. Here's a letter a young woman wrote me soon after she joined our community that may help explain what happens as we simply allow God to "tabernacle" with us wherever we are and whatever we are doing, all week long, inside and outside of formal gathering times:

> Hugh,
> I've been coming to Adullam for about a year now. Yesterday, during and after Lou's talk, I felt like I understood things a little better. And then going to the park afterwards to play volleyball with Laura, Sean, and some others, it hit me some more. Adullam is best defined by what its people are actively doing in their community. By just showing up on Sunday and trying to find your fit, the meaning of our community becomes more and more vague. And I think that's where some people get hung up and frustrated because they can't find such internal structure to lead them to their purpose. Adullam's people need to be active with the nonbelievers in their lives in order to discover what we are about. I like that things remain loose and sort of intangible within our "church." It forces people to make fruit outside our own walls, where Christ is trying to lead us. I'm glad I haven't gotten involved, per se, in the usual ways Christians find fulfillment in their churches. I've taken time to learn what Adullam is about, and I finally find myself in agreement with it.
> Thanks,
> Sue

We're finding that when we truly live, on purpose, as lights to the world around us, we really look forward to seeing each other at our gatherings. (There's so much to share—needs to communicate and good news to celebrate!) In other words, the more we scatter for mission to the world, the more meaning our gatherings have.

It might behoove us to rediscover the true "synagogue" experience of church again. The word *synagogue* simply means "gathering place." The earliest forms of synagogues can be traced back to the time of the Babylonian captivity, after the first temple was destroyed by Nebuchadnezzar. Just as early African American slave communities creatively formed underground worship houses and makeshift altars, so did the early Hebrews. They were led by common community instead of separatist clergy. By nature of the danger of meeting together, people had to decentralize the formal place of worship to back alleys and hidden caves. Synagogues were the "churches of the common people"—gathering places where they could support one another in prayer, shared study of Scripture, and simple encouragement to keep on with the faith.

Of Xboxes and Burning Bushes

So how do we find sacred and holy ground? Quite simply, you just have to look for it.

You may have heard the story of Moses and the burning bush. In a nutshell, Moses was herding sheep one day when he saw a bush on fire, only the bush stayed intact; it wasn't being consumed. Curious, he paused for a better look, and at this point God called him by name. Moses said, "Here I am" (Exod. 3:4). God warned him not to come any closer but to take off his sandals because "you are standing on holy ground" (Exod. 3:5 NLT).

So tell me, what made the difference between the soil that was suddenly deemed holy and the soil that the sheep had been grazing on, walking on, and making piles of sheep dung on just minutes before? The difference was that God appeared, and then Moses paused and walked toward the fire of holy activity. Elizabeth Barrett Browning described so lyrically how we all walk on sacred and holy ground, but some see it and worship while others, sheeplike, never look up or open their spiritual eyes and simply continue to see dirt, grass, and berries instead of flames of holy fire at our fingertips:

> Earth's crammed with heaven
> And every common bush afire with God;
> But only he who sees, takes off his shoes,
> The rest sit round it and pluck blackberries.[1]

Several months ago I was training some church planters from Phoenix. One pastor came up to me and spoke of his misery in trying to get a church full of temple worshipers to learn synagogue ways. He said, "I just don't know what to do. I can't take it anymore. The people just won't or can't get their focus off of the building and what they think should be happening inside it." Not being the most sensitive of coaches, I asked, "Why don't you just leave?" To my surprise, he stared for a moment, then started sharing how a new church is forming around his son's Xbox group. It seems he had challenged his son to simply play his video game when he (the pastor) brought some of his new friends, goths who were curious about Christ, to their home. Whether it was the call of God or just his son's dogged determination to play, the pastor filled his home that next Friday night with forty of his little Xboxers. He shared how his wife was connecting with a bunch of forgotten kids and how his family home had become holy ground.

Sometimes we really overthink this stuff. Here was a pastor pulling his hair out, trying to figure out the key to getting his parishioners to take the mission of God more seriously, when right in his own living room was a burning bush! He was naturally leading by example, and simply sharing this story with his people might be one place to begin helping them see what synagogue can look like in everyday life. Sacred space is all around! Just look for it, pause, notice it, and share it. People love stories, so as they happen in your life and community, share them. Encourage others to go and do likewise. Over time an excitement and magnetic quality grows around a life that is focused on "going out and being with" that adds a much-needed balance to "gathering and huddling in."

Intentionality in Creating Holy Ground

Even though holy ground or sacred space will show itself if we look for it, sometimes we the church need to help create it. If we pick up anything from Jesus, it is that he went looking for ways to take the good things of God out into the streets. Healings were done out in public; teaching was on hillsides and in rooms late at night; worship was obediently hearing and obeying what his Father was asking him to do moment by moment; shepherding and pastoral care were in the context of real life; collection and distribution of money to help bless and take care of practical needs happened spontaneously; and even leadership training, ministry practice, and prayer were done "along the way" or late at night in a garden. Everything was "out there" in the context of normal, everyday life. We may find a completely different experience of church if we quit looking for most everything to happen under the roof of the big house!

When you begin to see your normal life as full of opportunities for creating sacred space no matter what you're doing, it can become holy if you pay just a bit more attention and let God show up in it. If you are a doctor, lawyer, social worker, police officer, fireman, government employee, masseuse, beautician, stay-at-home mom, artist, musician, educator, minister, financial planner, real estate agent, or contractor of any kind, you are providing services that can bring a little of heaven to earth every day. Sometimes, if I'm feeling stressed, I go get a haircut. For some reason, just taking twenty minutes to forget about life, read a magazine, and have some stranger shampoo my balding head ministers to my soul like nothing else. Don't belittle the job you are doing. It's how God is going to use you to bless the world, if you pay attention and allow it to happen.

Sacred Space and Persecution

I'm not one of those "new-agey" Christians who think everywhere is church, but I do think that whenever the church—that is, you and me and maybe a few friends—is present in the normal flow of life, sacred space will be revealed.

If we are to be persecuted, let it be for the right reasons. We have too many folks slapping metaphorical bumper stickers on our foreheads declaring, "I'm an Obnoxious Christian and You'll Go to Hell if You Don't Become One Too." Do not come whining to me if you are being a Jerk for Jesus and people either don't respond or respond in anger. You are not being persecuted for righteousness' sake. Most likely you are being persecuted for being . . . well . . . a butthead. Yeah, a little harsh, but it beats being called a whitewashed tomb, a viper, or *raca* (which means fool)—all terms Jesus used for the proud religious folk who'd lost their compassionate hearts for God and people.

Be light. Be grace. Be the love of Jesus made flesh in the world. Love each other as Jesus loves you. Serve with joy. Create a holy space wherever you have opportunity. And then if you are persecuted for that, I promise to give you some empathy and love.

So what about the church? As you can see, Jesus's church is created, grown, and strengthened when his apprentices reveal his glory and sacred goodness in every nook and cranny of real life. Church is not where you go. Church is the visible reality of God's people dancing a new jig of kingdom life right alongside normal life.

Please don't give up on your church or leave. Find some friends and start being the church. Jesus died for his "bride," the church. The least we can do is stop bellyaching about her and try to make her as beautiful as Jesus intended her to be.

 To consider: How committed are you to helping build or beautify God's "church" as we've described it here? Would you consider giving your life for the church, just as Jesus did?

 To do: Grab 3–6 friends and begin an eight-week incarnational community experience. This is your best way to be the church, and it may actually begin to reform the church you're already associated with. (You can find infomation on these groups as described in *The Tangible Kingdom Primer* at www.missio.us. Click on Training, then Missional Community Leaders, register, watch the four videos, and away you go!)

"God, who made the world and everything in it, since He is Lord of heaven and earth, does not dwell in temples made with hands."

Acts 17:24 NKJV

12

PARTING SHOTS
FROM A SACRILEGIOUS MENTOR

It's Time to Make a Decision

In a beat-up old leather binding I have a copy of *My Utmost for His Highest*, written by Oswald Chambers. This well-known classic devotional has been a mainstay for me and countless thousands of Jesus lovers who have been inspired by the depth of this man's life and words. As an apprentice of his teaching, I used to frequent the most amazing bohemian bookstore called Powell's in Portland, Oregon, find an unused cavern between bookshelves, and read his thoughts.

On the way out, I always stopped to see if there were any incredible deals on used commentaries. Under a heavy pile I found a biography of Oswald Chambers written by a friend of his. I excitedly opened it to the section with all the pictures because I had never actually seen what he looked like. (Fit, young, happy. He was robust and outgoing until his sudden death at age forty-three when, as an army chaplain in Egypt during World War I, he died of a ruptured appendix, refusing to "take up a hospital bed" that a soldier might need.)

Then I read the front inside cover, and these words stuck with me and galvanized my lifelong respect not only for Chambers's words but for the way he lived his life. It said, "After meeting Oswald for the first time, I was shocked at what was then considered his undue levity. He was the most irreverent Reverend I had ever met!"[1]

Oswald, his wife (whom he affectionately nicknamed "Biddy"), and their young daughter lived in a bungalow near an English military base in Egypt during the war. The first Sunday they invited soldiers for afternoon tea, four hundred lonely servicemen showed up! Their small home was always open, and whenever anyone showed up unannounced for a meal, they were welcome. His wife never knew for certain how much to prepare, but somehow there was always enough. A close friend and fellow chaplain described the supper parties at the bungalow as "taking place with such hilarity as might have shocked the respectably religious."[2]

Reading this, my curiosity about his ministry and my respect for his teaching soared. It was because of the life behind the words he lived—a life of hospitality, laughter, love, sacrifice, optimism, winsomeness of spirit, and a deep love for the Lord that was real and human, not stiff and staid.

I became inspired to live a life like his.

One of the things I have tried so hard to do in this book is help you see the real Jesus behind the red letter words in your Bible—to help you imagine who he was behind the scenes a bit and hope you find the real man. It's one thing to read someone's quotes and stories, and it is significant, no doubt. But it is something else to discover the way someone lived and behaved in daily life with family, friends, and outsiders.

At the end of John's Gospel he wrote, "Jesus did many other things as well. If every one of them were written down, I suppose that even the whole world would not have room for the books that would be written" (21:25).

What were all the other stories that could have been written? Well, I suppose there were a lot more healings, many more outcasts and degenerates loved on, more stories of Jesus bucking the system, and many other words of teaching. But there were, in three short years, undoubtedly also hundreds of private conversations, jokes, and hilarious stories. Maybe even a few stories Jesus might have asked his friends to keep to themselves.

We know that most of his first twelve apprentices died for him. He had them at hello and kept them to the end. Why? Jesus had such incredible followers not because of what he preached as much as who he was. They loved the man, and they had never experienced a love like his before. They followed him and adjusted their entire lives around his mission because his life was so inspiring. They were completely wrecked after meeting him and could not return to the routine, self-oriented lives they'd had before.

We also know that many people did not keep following him.

Maybe out of fear, or misunderstanding, or the religious pressure not to rock the boat, most left Jesus before they really got to know him. In a poignant story, after a crowd had walked away from Jesus, he looked at his own, his closest buddies, the ones who knew the man behind his teaching so well, and asked, "Do you want to leave, too?" (John 6:67 NCV).

In truth he was asking them if they wanted to return to religion, to nebulous faith, or to a godless secular existence. He wanted them to know that if they followed him, they'd have to leave all three behind. Could they pay that cost? Did they want the benefits?

As Jesus asks you to start your apprenticeship, you too will have to leave something behind.

I can clearly remember four times in my life when I heard Jesus say, "Are you going to leave, too?" And each time I had to leave something behind to follow him.

The first was when I was a senior in high school. My parents' marriage was on the rocks, and my oldest sister was in a state mental hospital. I got a call that a family member

215

needed to drive down to deal with her and her difficult setback. To give my parents a break, I left a party I was at and drove down to handle the trauma. On this drive I heard a clear call to ministry and that this would be the first of many times I'd need to give up doing something easy to do something needed and meaningful.

The second time I felt Jesus asking me if I was willing to follow him more deeply was the day I proposed to Cheryl. I'd met Cheryl the previous year on a triple date. She was not my date that night, and I called my buddy afterward and said, "Dude, why didn't you hook me up with the other gal?"

He mentioned her great character and work with Young Life, but he also mentioned Cheryl had been married before and had a four-year-old son. As soon as he told me that, I said, "Yep, not interested." Six months later I saw Cheryl again at my friend's wedding. She looked familiar, but I didn't recognize her as the same girl. Being drawn to the way she looked in a black-and-white polka-dot dress, I inquired again, and he said, "Yep, same girl. You remember, the one who has a son. And I should probably mention that her son has severe epilepsy." Again I said, "Oh, yeah. Not interested in being a dad right now."

A month later I was walking down a picturesque Oregon beach. The sun was going down, the colors of the sunset were gorgeously romantic, and the warm breeze wisped over my face. I turned to my companion—Dennis!—and said, "Dude, this is the last Friday night I'm going to spend on a romantic beach with another guy!" Just a few weeks later I finally called Cheryl. We dated for three months, which was traditionally the time it took me to be willing to hold a girl's hand, and six months after that we were married.

Why was my decision to take her out so long in coming? One thing and one thing only: I didn't want to give up my life. I knew I was supposed to marry her and be Ryan's father from our first coffee date. The quality of her life since she had come to faith in Christ was obvious and inspiring. She had held down good jobs while hourly dealing with Ryan's intense seizures. She was tougher than anyone I had ever met. She was honest and real, optimistic and, yes, hot! But my attraction wasn't just some romantic, pubescent, hormonal rant. I literally knew that her life was supposed to be my life. It was as clear a spiritual call as I've ever had. I had fear; I knew what it would mean for me. I recognized that with Ryan's severe epilepsy, with nightly events I've described in detail, my life would forever be altered. My selfish desires for my life, although not totally wiped out, would be tested every day and night.

The third time Jesus said to me, "Do you want to leave, too?" was in a New York pub with a waitress named Fiona. For those of you who haven't read this story from my first book, *The Tangible Kingdom*, here is the CliffsNotes version. I, a burned-out pastor at the time, went into a New York Irish pub with some mates who were helping me train other pastors. I met Fiona, a burned-out Catholic from Belfast, who took a hankering to my description of the kingdom. Next thing I knew, she had invited other waiters to come listen. This experience left me babbling to myself on the curb. I could not get out of ministry; I could not escape the call. I realized that people are still drawn to the good news of the kingdom even though they may be completely done with the bad news of religion. I had a choice: stay jaded, disconnect from church, and be done with it, or reengage and relearn a whole new way to be in ministry.

The last call came a little while after Fiona jacked up my intentions to leave ministry. At this point we were in Denver, our new home base, and I planned to travel to speak to and train pastors but stay away from messing up our peaceful life by pastoring an actual church again. But one friendship led to another, conversations about Jesus happened with neighbors and at coffee shops, and one night Cheryl and I looked up at thirty people jammed into our living room talking about God. One gal asked, "Is this my church?"

I looked at Cheryl across the room and clearly saw her eyes communicate, "You'd better not say yes!" Then I looked at Matt, who was my partner in training pastors, and saw the same look: "Don't even go there, Hugh." Thinking quickly on my feet, I said, "Umm, no, this is not your church, this is your . . . hmm . . . faith community . . . yeah . . . your faith community."

"Well," the gal said, "I have come to faith, so aren't I supposed to have a church?"

Again thinking quickly, I answered, "Well, if we were to become a church, it would be different. A church would happen if we all decide to go on mission for God together. So far, Matt and his wife Maren and Cheryl and I have been on mission—creating time and opportunity to help you figure out life in the kingdom as Jesus taught it. We open up our home, we buy food and wine, we throw cool parties, we try to give our time to mentor you, and so on. If you all decide to be a church, you'll have to join us in doing that for others. You'll have to die to your own lives like we have."

Yeah, that'll scare them out of doing church, I thought to myself. The next week, they all decided they wanted to die with us, more or less. I was poised to do some more back-pedaling since I had no natural desire to start a church again, but something felt oddly, inexplicably right about this. I did have some great reservations, but since the Fiona moment, I knew God was up to something, so this moment served as my last "Will you continue to follow me?" call from God.

Whereas religion only calls you once ("I'm Catholic," "I go to First Baptist," "I'm a spiritual person"), apprenticeship is continual. You'll hear the general ongoing clarion call daily. And over your lifetime—whether you're a pastor, Sunday school teacher, or unpaid saint cleverly disguised as a plumber, golf pro, or nurse—there may be ten to twenty times you sense the call cutting you to the core of your own self-absorption and self-reliance. These calls will force you to walk the plank of faith again. You'll feel God's loving gaze revealing aspects of your life that limit his ability to use you, and you'll watch him clean those up and get you ready for service. You'll find your faith taking you to new levels you didn't know existed.

Where Apprenticeship Starts

In those moments I described, God's call pushed me beyond where I wanted to go. The disciples faced the same . . . or worse. My guess is that every day they followed Jesus, they had moments when they thought about returning to the lake to fish or heading back to tent making or tax collecting. Surely they were often on their knees with fear about what the next day with Jesus would cost them. I've already alluded to one palpable moment of decision which is recorded for us.

Many followers had just left Jesus when they heard what it might cost them. He wheeled around to his closest friends and asked, "Do you want to leave, too?" (John 6:67 NCV).

The would-be disciples now had their moment.

They could go back to their mommies or they could go on with Jesus. Peter's response is interesting: "Lord, who would we go to? You have the words that give eternal life" (John 6:68 NCV). Why didn't they ask Jesus details about where he was going? Why didn't they negotiate a compromise or ask if they could come and go as their schedules allowed? Why didn't they just take the out he offered?

One reason.

They loved him!

Although the disciples probably couldn't formulate their passion for this person into a logical argument, it was undeniably there. Certain distinctive relationships move us to act differently, love more deeply, and risk boldly. Such was Jesus's effect upon the apprentices. They did not want the sort of life they once had apart from him. They'd been ruined for the ordinary. What they saw in him transcended everything they hoped to get out of this world. And when push came to shove, they just couldn't leave him. He had the secret—the words of eternal life.

Most of us find it fairly easy to sign up to follow Jesus. But once you get the handbook on the cost of becoming his apprentice—or becoming *like* him—your heart will race, your breathing may be labored, and your mind will expand in ways you never thought possible. It's intense.

What is your answer to the question Jesus poses: "Do you want to leave, too?"

If you choose to jump into the pool of kingdom life, I can only tell you that it will be the most exhilarating, heart-expanding, heartbreaking, life-on-the-edge choice you will ever make. As Jesus himself said in the Beatitudes,

> You're blessed when you're at the end of your rope.
> With less of you there is more of God and his rule.
> You're blessed when you feel you've lost what is most
>   dear to you. Only then can you be embraced by
>   the One most dear to you.
> You're blessed when you're content with just who
>   you are—no more, no less. That's the moment you
>   find yourselves proud owners of everything that
>   can't be bought.
> You're blessed when you've worked up a good appe-
>   tite for God. He's food and drink in the best meal
>   you'll ever eat.
> You're blessed when you care. At the moment of
>   being "care-full," you find yourselves cared for.
> You're blessed when you get your inside world—your
>   mind and heart—put right. Then you can see God
>   in the outside world.
> You're blessed when you can show people how to co-
>   operate instead of compete or fight. That's when
>   you discover who you really are, and your place in
>   God's family.
> You're blessed when your commitment to God pro-
>   vokes persecution. The persecution drives you even
>   deeper into God's kingdom.

Not only that—count yourselves blessed every time people put you down or throw you out or speak lies about you to discredit me. What it means is that the truth is too close for comfort and they are uncomfortable. You can be glad when that happens—give a cheer, even!—for though they don't like it, I do! And all heaven applauds. And know that you are in good company. My prophets and witnesses have always gotten into this kind of trouble. (Matt. 5:3–12 Message)

These are incredible promises for any and all apprentices!

Although following Jesus leaves you with some scars, I wouldn't trade in this life for anything, and as wild a ride as it's been, this life has been as meaningful as I could ever imagine. So I don't mind inviting you into it with me.

Where do you begin? Well, on the practical level, I think you should have this conversation with a few more friends. Jesus never called people to follow him by themselves. He knew that life in the kingdom was and still is only available for those committed to community with other apprentices. So you may want to read this book again with a few more friends, and if you want to push forward, then I'd recommend a subversive little book called *The Tangible Kingdom Primer*, which is an eight-week spiritual formation guide for would-be apprentices (available at http://www.missio.us). Thousands of people are now using this primer to learn to make the kingdom tangible, and we'd love to have you with us. If enough of us heed the call, it will change the very essence, reputation, and influence of what Jesus calls his church!

Tipping Point

We're all concerned about God and his church, and especially whether or not the mundane Western Christian experience will change. Well, I believe it is changing. Recently I heard that in any situation where you have competing experiences and worldviews, when you get about 15 percent of any culture to adopt a new paradigm, that paradigm will eventually bleed through, infect, and infiltrate the entire movement. Fifteen percent seems to be the tipping point.

I've also heard that if each person changes the lives of three people and those three people in turn change three people's lives, we can change the whole world in our lifetime. I envision a day when God's people, Jesus's apprentices, can't keep people away from their countercultural life of the kingdom— a day when the church is so beautiful that people will be lining up to be a part of her movement and mission.

I hope I've changed the minds of at least three of you.

 To consider: I invite you to revisit the letter you began to draft at the beginning of the book. Based on some new insight you might have gained from this book, if you had one page to try to describe Jesus to the people you care most about, what would you say?

"When the heart sees what God wants . . . the body must be willing to be spent for that cause alone."

Oswald Chambers

APPENDIX

A Brief History of Communion

The story of the Lord's Supper actually began as the Lord ... had supper. Three of the four Gospels show Jesus holding his last meal with the men he'd been preparing to carry on his mission of saving the world (see Matt. 26:20–30; Mark 14:16–26; Luke 22:13–38). All three make specific mention that this meal was on the eve of Passover. The Passover is significant to our understanding the meaning of communion because it exposes the specific meal practices upon which Jesus was building his new communion practices. Within the weeklong vigil were many dinners, celebrations, remembrances, and religious ceremonies.

In fact, there were three Jewish meal practices. One was the Passover Seder meal, in which blessings were made over cups of wine before and after the meal. Another was called kiddush, a ceremony where thanksgivings were recited while bread and a cup of wine were passed around the room. The last was called the chaburah, but it was not the name of a rite but actually the name of a group of male friends who would meet for important religious celebrations and give formal blessings over food and wine, long prayers of thanksgiving, and a benediction or singing of psalms. All Jews would have been familiar with these intricate meal practices.

The Greeks and Romans also had elaborate spiritual ceremonies that centered on the common meal and included blessings. One in particular exposes the fact that eating flesh and drinking blood wasn't that strange of an idea in ancient times. The most well-known practice centered around Dionysus, who was Zeus's son. He was considered the god of the vine. Whereas other Greek gods were separate from humanity, Dionysus was considered the most accessible to the normal man. Dionysian followers would take part in what was called the "feast of raw flesh," where they would drink a goat's blood and eat the flesh of the animal right from the carcass. They believed consuming both the flesh and blood made them one with their god.

Some scholars believe that this feast was what Jesus was alluding to when he shocked his would-be followers with the call to "eat his flesh and drink his blood" (see John 6:54). As Jesus refers to himself as the "bread of life" (John 6:35), he's again not sharing some strange new concept. He's simply building upon the common belief of both Jews and Gentiles, that he is the essence of life, sustenance, and celebration. He is now to be the "toast" of the town.

After Jesus set the model, the earliest faith communities continued the Eucharist in both formal and informal ways. Much of the church was dispersed and unsanctioned because of persecution, so communion was often held in a more "underground" fashion. The church didn't have a formal hierarchy, and thus people took communion in the context of their normal meal practices.

Communion: A Significant Meal Practice, Not an Institution of the Church

One thing to point out is that Jesus was not instituting a new practice that would be unique to Christians or a certain strain of "serious Christians" as much as he was contextualizing a new faith inside their well-known meal practices. He used both Jewish and Gentile meal and celebration practices to draw people into a relational ceremony that would help them centralize Christ in their daily experience. Both sides of the religious spectrum were steeped in hospitality and the communal sharing of time, friends, and food. It was by this experience that Jesus asked his followers to remember him. To the Jewish folk, he was saying, "I want to be the toast of the town now." To the Gentile spiritualist, he was saying, "Just as you expected to become one with your pagan gods through eating their flesh and drinking their blood, you can become one with me through the same focus."

This understanding helps us see that Jesus never intended communion to become an ordinance of an institutional church. The church was just getting started at this time, and it wouldn't be until about three hundred years later, when the Roman leader Constantine came to faith, that this pure, meaningful celebration of faith and friendship would get co-opted into a formal rite.

Abusing Communion

"But Hugh," I hear you asking, "didn't Jesus worry about people taking communion with the wrong motives or wrong heart? Isn't that why both Catholic and Protestant churches try to ensure religious purity before someone takes it? Isn't it good to make sure people take it seriously?"

To be sure, part of the historical saga of communion is many abuses. As the practice grew, and especially as it began to link Gentiles, Greeks, and Romans into the church, their pagan and Jewish meal practices got out of hand.

Fear of ceremonial abuses was nothing new, of course, as we see it as far back as 800 BC. The prophet Amos denounced the exuberant social and spiritual gatherings and celebrations of Israel's upper class. He referred to their assemblies, feasts, music, ointments, wine, and reclining posture in a negative light. Apparently it symbolized lurid, hypocritical gatherings that were not pleasing to God (see Amos 5:21–24).

Another story obviously took place outside a church service but gives us some understanding of why communion began to be more formal. In AD 100, a major church leader named Ignatius of Antioch leveled these words about the agape love feasts (communion): "Let the Eucharist alone be considered valid which is celebrated in the presence of the bishop, or of him to whom he shall have entrusted it. . . . It is not lawful either to baptize or to hold a love-feast without the consent of the bishop."

Two hundred years later, when Constantine locked the door on the centralized church, love feasts were all but shut down as the church sought to control both insiders and outsiders. During the Middle Ages, between around AD 800–1000, the Eucharist was now completely in the hands of the pros: the ordained clergy. By then the number of Christians was exploding, mostly due to the fact that if you were Roman, you pretty much had to be a Christian (sort of like how if you move to Green Bay, you have to at least look like a Packers fan). Church buildings were now the focus, and church services replaced the informal home gatherings around meals. The church was made up of individuals coming to receive their religious rites instead of a community gathering around food, wine, and the simple remembrance of Jesus.

The church was now institutionalized, and communion became not only a meaningful sacrament of the church but also a deep line in the sand that categorized who was in and out. As is the case in any institutional box, even though fear of abuses may be warranted, the outcome tends toward either control, which often leads to the abuse of power, or excess in the opposite direction, where sin is not taken seriously. Both of these veil the true meaning. So it was with communion. The real meaning became either watered down or entrenched in a maze of man-made add-ons that rendered the true form or original purpose obscure. Later, in the age of Charlemagne, around AD 742–812, many non-Romans were being added to the church. Many people were baptized without what the church leaders deemed to be an adequate education. These factors and more eventually led to a complete chasm between clergy and laity because the priests ended up serving communion with their backs to the people, communicating that the local peasants were not as spiritual as the pros.

In this brief historical sketch you can see how the institutional church tried to bring correction to a "loose communion" but in the end swung the pendulum too far. Along the way, even in Protestant circles, most notably the eighteenth-century Pietists, communion retained the institutional constraints. Even though the Pietists brought back the formal "love feast," communion was something that had to be earned. People had to go through rigorous testing by the community to receive the elements. A vestige of this "in/out" mentality has remained in our common evangelical experience.

Although there were and always will be some abuses when peasants run their own spiritual practices, we have to fight against any Christian ritual that smacks of control, especially if it limits anyone from coming to Jesus for grace. When Jesus broke bread and gave wine to his friends, it was an extremely emotional and relational gift. He loved his buddies and wanted them to have an experience they would never forget. He knew that these men would be challenging the religions of the day and that their sacrilegious message would soon cost them their lives. Jews and Greeks would someday persecute the people of "the way," and thus Jesus centered his life in the hearts of his followers in the middle of a quiet, dimly lit room. Not only did Jesus not want to start a new ordinance of organized religion, but he meant for communion to be the tie that bound God's nonreligious, noninstitutional people together.

NOTES

Chapter 1 Sacrilegious Jesus

1. Michka Assayas, *Bono: in Conversation with Michka Assayas* (New York: Riverhead Books, 2005), 124–25.

Chapter 4 Open Your Mind, Enter the Kingdom

1. Emmett Fox, *The Sermon on the Mount* (New York: HarperCollins, 1989), 21.
2. Dallas Willard, *The Divine Conspiracy* (New York: HarperCollins, 1998), xiii.

Chapter 11 Of Xboxes and Burning Bushes

1. Elizabeth Barrett Browning, "Aurora Leigh," in The *Oxford Book of English Mystical Verse*, ed. D. H. S. Nicholson and A. H. E. Lee (Oxford: The Clarendon Press, 1917); Bartleby.com, 2000, http://www.bartleby.com/236.

Chapter 12 Parting Shots from a Sacrilegious Mentor

1. David McCasland, *Oswald Chambers: Abandoned to God* (Grand Rapids: Discovery House, 1993).
2. Ibid., 240.

Hugh Halter is a church planter, pastor, consultant, and missionary to the United States. He is the national director of Missio and is the lead architect of Adullam, a congregational network of missional communities in Denver, Colorado. He has coauthored *The Tangible Kingdom*, *The Tangible Kingdom Primer*, and *AND: The Gathered and Scattered Church*.

Organic Leadership
Neil Cole

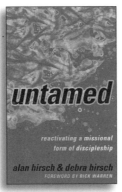

Untamed
Alan Hirsch and Debra Hirsch

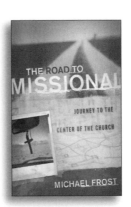

Right Here, Right Now
Alan Hirsch and Lance Ford

The Faith of Leap
Michael Frost and Alan Hirsch

The Road to Missional
Michael Frost

BakerBooks
a division of Baker Publishing Group
www.BakerBooks.com